THE
HABIT
PLAYBOOK

*Timeless Productivity Secrets from
History's Greatest Minds*

FELIX GRAYSON

MINDSPARK
PUBLISHING

To those who strive each day to grow, transform, and inspire—this book is for you. May your journey be guided by purpose, sustained by resilience, and illuminated by the power of habits.

"We are what we repeatedly do. Excellence, then, is not an act, but a habit."

— Aristotle

ABOUT STONED PHILOSOPHER

Welcome to the *Stoned Philosopher* series—where timeless wisdom meets the modern world.

Each book distills powerful lessons from history's greatest minds, leaders, and thinkers—transforming their ideas into practical insights for today's challenges.

From mastering habits, calm, and resilience to understanding success, leadership, and meaning, this collection invites you to think deeper, live wiser, and see life from new perspectives.

Whether you're exploring *Modern Zen*, uncovering *The Wisdom of Warriors*, or seeking clarity through *The Art of Perspective*, every title offers a journey toward self-mastery and understanding.

Discover the full *Stoned Philosopher* collection and more at **FelixGrayson.com**, home of **Mind-Spark Publishing**—where knowledge, philosophy, and storytelling come together to spark lifelong curiosity.

FelixGrayson.com 🔍

Wisdom isn't something we find—it's something we grow into.

Let the journey begin.

CONTENTS

CHAPTER 3: THE MORNING POWERHOUSE – STARTING THE DAY LIKE HISTORY'S GREATS

CHAPTER 4: THE KEYSTONE HABIT – UNLOCKING EXPONENTIAL GROWTH 92

INTRODUCTION: A JOURNEY OF TRANSFORMATION

Have you ever stopped to wonder how the smallest actions in your day ripple out to shape the person you are, the life you live, and the future you create? Perhaps it's the quiet moments: the way you start your morning, the words you choose when speaking to a friend, or the way you close your day. These seemingly insignificant decisions, repeated over time, form the backbone of your identity. They are your habits.

Habits are often invisible, woven so tightly into the fabric of daily life that we scarcely notice their existence. Yet they hold extraordinary power—power to transform, uplift, and propel us toward our greatest aspirations. This book is about harnessing that power, understanding it, and using it to create a life of growth, purpose, and fulfillment.

The Hidden Blueprint of Our Lives

Every great accomplishment, from the towering achievements of history's most revered figures to the quiet triumphs of personal growth, is underpinned by habits. Aristotle taught us that "We are what we repeatedly do. Excellence, then, is not an act, but a habit." His words remind us that greatness is not born of singular moments but of consistent, intentional action.

Consider the morning routines of some of history's greatest minds. Maya Angelou began her days with a disciplined writing habit, carving out space and time to create some of the most profound literary works of our age. Benjamin Franklin meticulously planned his mornings to cultivate virtues that aligned with his life's ambitions. These individuals understood that habits are not merely routines—they are the architecture of success, designed to align our daily actions with our highest goals.

But habits are not just about personal achievement. They are deeply connected to who we are as human beings. They shape our relationships, influence our communities, and even drive societal progress. The shared habits of a family create bonds of trust and love. The collective routines of a team foster unity and success. And the cultural habits of a society define its identity and future.

Why Habits Matter Now More Than Ever

We live in a world of constant change, where distractions are plentiful, and time feels like a fleeting resource. In such a fast-paced environment, habits provide a sense of stability and purpose. They ground us in our values and help us navigate life's uncertainties with resilience and clarity.

The past few years have shown us the fragility of routine and the importance of adaptability. The global pandemic disrupted lives and reshaped how we work, connect, and grow. Amid this chaos, many of us turned to habits—whether to find comfort in the familiar or to build new routines that helped us adapt to unprecedented challenges.

This book is a response to those challenges. It is a guide to understanding the profound role habits play in our lives and a roadmap for using them to create a life of intention and fulfillment.

Whether you are seeking to break free from unproductive patterns, build routines that align with your goals, or inspire collective growth within your community, the pages ahead will offer you the tools, insights, and inspiration to make it happen.

The Purpose of This Book

The *Habit Playbook* is not just a book about habits; it is a call to action. It is an invitation to look deeply at the routines that define your life and to ask, "Are these habits serving my highest purpose?"

In these chapters, we will explore the timeless wisdom of history's greatest minds and the cutting-edge science of behavior change. We will examine the habits that shaped leaders, thinkers, and innovators, uncovering the strategies that propelled them to greatness. We will delve into the neuroscience of habit formation, the psychology of motivation, and the art of resilience, offering you practical tools to apply these lessons in your own life.

Each chapter builds on the last, taking you on a

journey from understanding the fundamentals of habits to mastering the art of habit transformation. Along the way, you will discover:

- How to design habits that align with your values and goals.

- The power of keystone habits to create ripple effects in your life.

- Strategies for breaking free from bad habits and replacing them with positive ones.

- The role of collective habits in driving team and societal success.

- The importance of adaptability, reflection, and celebration in sustaining lifelong growth.

A Personal Invitation

Before we begin, I want to extend a personal invitation. This book is not a set of rigid rules or one-size-fits-all solutions. It is a conversation—a dialogue between the wisdom of the past, the insights of the present, and the possibilities of your future. It is meant to inspire curiosity, spark reflection, and empower you to take action.

As you read, I encourage you to approach each chapter with an open mind and a willingness to experiment. The lessons and practices shared here are not meant to be prescriptive but rather a starting point for your own exploration. Use them as tools to craft a life that reflects your unique values, aspirations, and potential.

The Journey Ahead

The journey of transformation begins with understanding. In the first chapters, we will explore the foundations of great habits—what they are, how they form, and why they matter. We will delve into the science behind habit formation and discover the hidden mechanisms that drive behavior.

From there, we will turn our attention to action: building better habits, breaking free from unproductive patterns, and mastering the art of resilience. You will learn how to create routines that align with your goals, sustain momentum through change, and celebrate progress along the way.

Finally, we will reflect on the bigger picture. Habits are not just about personal growth—they are about legacy. In the closing chapters, we will explore how the habits you cultivate today can inspire future generations and create a lasting impact on the world around you.

A Final Thought

As we embark on this journey together, remember that transformation is not about perfection—it is about progress. It is about showing up each day with intention, embracing the process of growth, and finding fulfillment in the journey itself.

In the words of Confucius, "The will to win, the desire to succeed, the urge to reach your full potential… these are the keys that will unlock the door to personal excellence." Habits are the key to that door. They are the tools we use to unlock our potential, one small action at a time.

Let this book be your guide, your companion, and your source of inspiration as you take the first step—and every step thereafter—on your journey of transformation.

Welcome to the *Habit Playbook*. Your next chapter begins now.

CHAPTER 1: FOUNDATIONS OF GREAT HABITS – THE BUILDING BLOCKS OF SUCCESS

Defining Habits – The Invisible Architect of Life

Habits are the invisible threads weaving through the fabric of our lives. These small, often unconscious actions guide our days, shaping not only who we are but who we aspire to become. Aristotle, one of history's most profound thinkers, famously asserted that "we are what we repeatedly do. Excellence, then, is not an act but a habit." In this deceptively simple statement lies a powerful truth: habits are the foundation upon which virtues, achievements, and legacies are built.

From the moment we wake up, our habits govern us. Some are deliberate—the morning stretch, the freshly brewed coffee, the short walk to clear the mind. Others operate in the background, unnoticed but deeply influential. Together, they create the patterns of our lives, forming a personal rhythm that defines our character. Over time, these patterns compound, their effects multiplying until they become the distinguishing features of our success—or our stagnation.

Aristotle saw habits as the building blocks of virtue. To him, becoming virtuous wasn't an inherent state but a practice, a series of repeated actions leading to moral and intellectual excellence. Virtue, he taught, is cultivated through disciplined, habitual behavior, whether it's honesty, courage, or temperance. For Aristotle, habits were more than mundane routines; they were the tools that allowed individuals to fulfill their potential, aligning their actions with their highest ideals. By consciously choosing good habits, we not only refine our character but also set the stage for extraordinary achievements.

The power of small, consistent habits is exemplified throughout history. Consider the case of Benjamin Franklin, one of America's Founding Fathers. Franklin is often celebrated for his monumental achievements as a statesman, inventor, and philosopher, but behind his brilliance lay a carefully curated set of daily habits. Franklin's famous "13 virtues" included principles such as temperance, industry, and humility, each paired with a specific practice. He meticulously tracked his adherence to these virtues in a notebook, understanding that greatness was not the result of fleeting inspiration but of consistent, deliberate action. Franklin's life reminds us that even the most modest habits, when aligned with a larger purpose, can fuel greatness.

Another striking example comes from Mahatma Gandhi. Known for his role in leading India to independence, Gandhi's life was marked by simplicity and steadfastness. One of his most enduring habits was his daily spinning of cotton on the charkha, a small hand-operated spinning wheel. While seemingly trivial, this act symbolized Gandhi's commitment to self-reliance and his rejection of colonial oppression. By weaving thread each day, he not only created a practical resource but also reinforced the principles of independence and equality that he sought to instill in his people. Through a single, repetitive action, Gandhi transformed a habit into a statement of profound political and moral significance.

These historical figures teach us that habits are not merely tools for personal convenience but vehicles for self-transformation. Whether it's Franklin refining his virtues or Gandhi embodying resilience through simplicity, their lives demonstrate the profound impact of conscious, intentional habits. The essence of their wisdom lies in understanding that small, consistent actions, repeated over time, can lead to extraordinary outcomes.

Modern psychology supports this ancient insight. Research shows that habits form through repetition, becoming automatic responses to specific cues in our environment. This process occurs in the basal ganglia, a part of the brain responsible for pattern recognition and routine behaviors. By understanding the science of habit formation, we gain the ability to influence our behavior at its root, transforming actions that were once sporadic into consistent, life-enhancing practices.

For today's reader, the challenge is not merely to adopt new habits but to choose them wisely. Each habit represents a small commitment, a step toward shaping the person we wish to become. The act of selecting which habits to cultivate can be a deeply personal, almost philosophical exercise. It's not about adopting routines that work for others; it's about finding those small, repeatable actions that align with our values, our dreams, and our vision for the future.

To start, reflect on the actions you repeat daily. Which ones serve you, and which hold you back? Are there small, seemingly insignificant habits— such as checking your phone first thing in the morning or skipping meals—that may be shaping your life in unintended ways? Conversely, are there simple practices you could adopt, like journaling or taking a mindful moment, that could subtly but profoundly transform your outlook and productivity?

Habits are the architects of our lives, silent yet powerful. By choosing them deliberately and aligning them with our values, we begin to wield their transformative potential. Just as Franklin tracked his virtues and Gandhi spun cotton, so too can we design routines that reflect and reinforce our highest ideals. In doing so, we not only create a life of purpose and productivity but also move closer to Aristotle's vision of excellence—a state achieved not by chance but by habit.

The journey to mastery begins here, with an understanding of habits as the invisible architects of who we are. When chosen with intention, these small, repeated actions can lead to profound personal transformation, paving the way for a life not just of success, but of significance.

Why Habits Matter – The Compound Effect in Action

The true power of habits lies in their ability to compound over time, transforming small actions into monumental results. Imagine a single drop of water carving through rock—not in a day, nor in a year, but over centuries. This is the essence of the compound effect: the gradual, invisible build-up of effort that eventually reshapes the world around it. Habits operate much the same way, shaping not only individuals but entire societies.

The compound effect is best understood through the lens of incremental growth. Each small action, seemingly insignificant in isolation, adds up over time to produce extraordinary outcomes. Consider the act of reading one page of a book each day. In a week, you've read seven pages. In a year, that becomes 365. Over a decade, you've read dozens of books—not by making a monumental effort but by consistently showing up, day after day. The same principle applies to habits, which, when aligned with purpose, create exponential growth that far outweighs the initial investment of time and energy.

One of the most powerful tools for harnessing the compound effect is **habit stacking,** a concept rooted in the idea of building new behaviors onto existing routines. The key to habit stacking lies in its simplicity: you take something you already do automatically and attach a new habit to it. For example, after brushing your teeth in the morning, you might spend two minutes practicing mindfulness or reciting affirmations. Over time, these small additions become second nature, seamlessly integrating into your day without requiring a conscious decision. The result is a cascade of positive actions that build momentum and reinforce one another.

Benjamin Franklin, a master of productivity and personal growth, understood the power of incremental effort long before the term "habit stacking" was coined. Franklin's daily rituals were a testament to his belief in the compound effect. Each morning, he asked himself, "What good shall I do this day?" and in the evening, "What good have I done today?" These simple reflections were accompanied by deliberate practices aimed at cultivating his famous "13 virtues," such as temperance, frugality, and humility. By consistently tracking his progress, Franklin ensured that his small, daily actions aligned with his broader goals. Over the course of his life, these habits became the bedrock of his remarkable achievements.

Franklin's approach highlights another critical aspect of habits: their ability to extend beyond the individual and influence society as a whole. When personal habits align with a larger vision, they inspire collective action, creating a ripple effect that transforms communities. This dynamic can be seen in the environmental movement of the 20th century. Small, individual actions—recycling a can, reducing water usage, or planting a tree—gradually coalesced into a global shift in awareness about sustainability. These habits, multiplied across millions of people, have reshaped policies, industries, and cultural norms, proving that even the smallest actions, when compounded, can drive monumental change.

The impact of habits on societal structures is not a modern phenomenon. Historical movements often began with the disciplined habits of a few committed individuals. Take the civil rights movement, for example, where acts as simple as refusing to give up a seat on a bus or organizing a lunch counter sit-in became catalysts for systemic change. These actions were not spontaneous; they were the result of deliberate preparation and practice. Rosa Parks, often celebrated as the spark that ignited the Montgomery Bus Boycott, was no stranger to activism. Her decision to remain seated that fateful day was grounded in years of habitual resistance to injustice, cultivated through her involvement in the civil rights movement. Her seemingly small act was the embodiment of the compound effect, triggering a series of events that transformed the landscape of American society.

The beauty of the compound effect is its universality. Whether it's building personal habits or fostering societal change, the principle remains the same: consistency over time produces exponential results. However, this principle also comes with a cautionary tale. Just as good habits compound into extraordinary outcomes, bad habits can lead to destructive consequences. Consider the story of a once-thriving business that collapses under the weight of complacency or a relationship that erodes due to repeated neglect. These negative patterns, often unnoticed in the moment, accumulate over time until their effects become undeniable.

For the individual, the challenge is to become aware of which habits are compounding positively and which are eroding progress. This requires a degree of self-reflection and honesty that is both humbling and empowering. Start by examining your daily routines: Are there small actions that, while seemingly harmless, are steering you away from your goals? Conversely, are there habits you could adopt, however minor, that might bring you closer to the life you envision?

The magic of the compound effect lies in its gradual, almost imperceptible nature. It does not demand perfection or monumental leaps; it requires only consistency. This is both its greatest strength and its greatest challenge. The slow pace of progress can be discouraging, but it is precisely this pace that ensures the changes are lasting. The tree that grows slowly has roots that run deep, able to weather storms and sustain growth for generations.

Habits matter because they embody this principle. They are the tiny drops of water that carve through rock, the pages that fill a book, the steps that build a journey. By understanding and embracing the compound effect, we unlock the potential for transformation not only in ourselves but in the world around us. The challenge, then, is to choose our habits wisely, knowing that each small action today has the power to shape our tomorrow.

The Habit Loop – Understanding the Science Behind Change

Every habit, whether beneficial or detrimental, operates within a predictable framework known as the habit loop. This loop consists of three interconnected components: the cue, the routine, and the reward. Understanding this cycle is essential for mastering habits, as it provides the tools to consciously create new behaviors or disrupt patterns that no longer serve us. Rooted in psychology and neuroscience, the habit loop

serves as a blueprint for how our brains automate actions, freeing up mental resources for
more complex tasks.

The first element of the habit loop is the **cue**, a
trigger that signals the brain to initiate a behavior. Cues can take many forms: a time of
day, a specific location, an emotional state, or
even an interaction with another person. For
example, the sight of your running shoes by the
door might cue you to lace up and go for a jog.
Conversely, the sound of your phone buzzing
might prompt you to check notifications, even
when it distracts from your priorities. The cue
sets the stage for the routine to follow, acting as
a signpost for what comes next.

The second component is the **routine**, the behavior itself. This is the action repeated in response to the cue, whether it's productive, like
sitting down to meditate after waking up, or
unproductive, like mindlessly scrolling social
media whenever you feel bored. The routine
becomes the heart of the habit, and its effectiveness depends on the context established by the
cue and the motivation provided by the reward.

The final element is the **reward**, the payoff that reinforces the habit. Rewards can be tangible, like the satisfaction of checking off an item on your to-do list, or intangible, like the feeling of calm after completing a yoga session. Rewards signal to the brain that the action was beneficial, encouraging the repetition of the behavior in the future. Over time, the cue becomes tightly associated with the reward, making the routine feel automatic.

One historical figure who exemplified mastery of the habit loop was Charles Darwin. As he developed his groundbreaking theory of evolution, Darwin relied on a carefully structured daily routine to maintain his focus and productivity. His mornings were dedicated to writing and reflection, spurred by the cue of early sunlight and a quiet workspace. The routine of consistent writing became a ritual, and the reward was the progress he saw in his work—a motivation that reinforced his dedication. Darwin's methodical approach to his day allowed him to produce one of the most significant scientific works of all time, proving that understanding and leveraging the habit loop can yield extraordinary results.

Modern neuroscience reveals how the habit loop operates at a biological level. Habits are stored in the basal ganglia, a part of the brain responsible for pattern recognition and automation. This system evolved as a survival mechanism, enabling humans to conserve mental energy by automating repetitive tasks. For instance, once you've learned to ride a bicycle, the habit becomes so deeply ingrained that you no longer need to consciously think about balancing or pedaling—it simply happens. This efficiency is a gift, but it also presents a challenge: once a habit is formed, it becomes resistant to change.

The resilience of habits can be both a blessing and a curse. Good habits, like brushing your teeth or exercising regularly, provide long-term benefits with minimal effort. However, bad habits, like smoking or procrastination, can become deeply ingrained, making them difficult to break. The key to transformation lies in recognizing and reshaping the habit loop. By identifying the cue, altering the routine, and maintaining the reward, it's possible to rewire even the most stubborn habits.

To put this theory into practice, consider a practical exercise in observing your own habit loops. Start by selecting a habit you'd like to change or reinforce. Over the course of a week, take note of the specific cues that trigger the behavior. Is it a time of day, like late afternoon when you reach for a sugary snack? Or an emotional state, like stress that leads to mindless online shopping? Write down these observations without judgment, focusing solely on identifying the pattern.

Next, examine the routine. What exactly do you do in response to the cue? Break the behavior down into its smallest components to gain clarity. Then, reflect on the reward. What satisfaction or relief does the routine provide? By understanding the payoff, you can begin to experiment with alternative routines that satisfy the same need. For instance, if stress drives you to snack on sweets, consider replacing that routine with a short walk or a few minutes of deep breathing. The reward—reduced stress—remains, but the behavior becomes healthier and more intentional.

The beauty of the habit loop lies in its universality. It applies not only to individuals but also to groups and organizations. Shared habits within teams or communities often follow a collective habit loop, where cues, routines, and rewards align to drive collective behavior. Consider the rituals of military units, where the sound of a bugle (cue) triggers the disciplined actions of assembling and saluting (routine), reinforced by a sense of camaraderie and purpose (reward). These collective habits, rooted in the same principles as individual ones, underscore the power of structure and repetition in shaping outcomes.

Understanding the habit loop is not just an exercise in self-awareness—it's a strategy for empowerment. By recognizing the patterns that govern our actions, we gain the ability to rewrite them. The habit loop becomes a tool for change, a means of consciously crafting the life we desire. Whether you're seeking to break free from unproductive routines or establish new ones that propel you forward, the principles of the habit loop offer a clear and actionable path. Armed with this knowledge, you can transform habits from invisible forces of inertia into intentional agents of growth and success.

Setting the Foundation – Start Small to Win Big

Great achievements often have humble beginnings. In the grand tapestry of human history, some of the most profound transformations have emerged not from sweeping, dramatic actions but from small, consistent efforts. Habits, like seeds, begin small yet hold the potential to grow into towering structures of success. Setting the foundation for meaningful change begins with embracing this truth: start small, remain consistent, and watch the results compound over time.

The power of small, consistent actions lies in their accessibility. Grand ambitions, while inspiring, can often feel overwhelming and out of reach. By contrast, small actions are manageable and repeatable. They require minimal mental and emotional energy to initiate, which is precisely why they are so effective. Over time, these small actions build momentum, eventually leading to outcomes far beyond their modest beginnings.

Consider the daily walks of Mahatma Gandhi.

Known for his leadership in India's struggle for independence, Gandhi's life was punctuated by simple, deliberate habits that reinforced his values. Among these was his daily practice of walking, an act he believed was essential for both physical and mental clarity. What may seem like an ordinary routine carried profound symbolism for Gandhi. Each step was a reaffirmation of his commitment to self-reliance and his connection to the people he served. Over time, these walks became a powerful metaphor for the journey of independence itself: a series of small, steady steps that collectively reshaped the destiny of a nation.

The lesson here is clear: small habits can serve as the bedrock for larger goals. They create a foundation upon which greater actions are built, much like a sturdy base supports a towering structure. Starting small does not diminish the magnitude of a goal; rather, it provides the stability necessary to achieve it.

Science supports this principle. The psychology of habit formation emphasizes the importance of reducing barriers to entry. The smaller and more achievable a habit, the more likely it is to stick. This concept, known as the "two-minute rule," suggests that any new habit should take no longer than two minutes to complete in its initial stages. The simplicity of this approach ensures that even the most daunting goals can be broken down into manageable steps. For instance, if your goal is to write a book, the habit might begin with writing a single sentence each day. While this may seem trivial, it sets the wheels of momentum in motion, making it easier to build upon the habit over time.

Another powerful example of starting small comes from the life of Florence Nightingale, the founder of modern nursing. Nightingale's groundbreaking work in improving hospital sanitation began with seemingly modest actions, such as ensuring patients had access to fresh air and clean bedding. These small but consistent changes, implemented during her time in the Crimean War, significantly reduced mortality rates and revolutionized healthcare practices. Nightingale's work illustrates how incremental improvements, when applied consistently, can lead to transformative outcomes.

For readers seeking to set the foundation for

their own habits, the key lies in identifying "starter habits" that are both meaningful and achievable. A starter habit serves as the entry point for a larger routine, much like the first step of a staircase. To identify a suitable starter habit, consider the following framework:

1. **Align with Your Values**: Choose a habit that resonates with your long-term goals and personal values. For instance, if health is a priority, a starter habit might be as simple as drinking a glass of water each morning.

2. **Keep It Manageable**: The habit should be small enough to complete without resistance. If you aim to meditate daily, start with one minute instead of twenty. The ease of completion ensures consistency, which is the foundation of growth.

3. **Tie It to an Existing Routine**: Attach the new habit to an existing one, leveraging the principle of habit stacking. For example, if you brush your teeth every night, use that moment as a cue to practice gratitude by thinking of one positive thing from your day.

By beginning with starter habits, you create a domino effect, where the completion of one small action paves the way for the next. This approach not only builds confidence but also reinforces a sense of progress, no matter how incremental. Over time, these small habits evolve into larger routines, much like a single snowflake accumulating with others to form a mighty avalanche.

The story of the Wright brothers offers another inspiring example of the power of incremental action. Before achieving their groundbreaking flight, Orville and Wilbur Wright spent years testing small adjustments to their designs. Each tweak, however minor, brought them closer to their ultimate goal. Their success was not the result of a single, grand invention but of countless small experiments, each building on the last. Their journey underscores the idea that progress is often measured not in leaps but in steps.

To set the foundation for success, it's essential to embrace the idea of starting small and staying consistent. This approach not only makes goals feel more attainable but also fosters the discipline necessary for long-term growth. Remember, every towering oak tree began as a small acorn, and every great achievement starts with a single, deliberate action.

In setting your foundation, focus not on the size of the action but on its direction. Are your habits moving you closer to your goals or further away? By taking small, consistent steps in the right direction, you build the habits that will ultimately define your success. Through this process, you gain the confidence to tackle greater challenges, secure in the knowledge that even the smallest actions, when repeated over time, can lead to extraordinary outcomes.

This is the essence of setting the foundation for great habits: start small, stay consistent, and let the power of incremental growth carry you toward your vision of success.

CHAPTER 2: THE SCIENCE OF PRODUCTIVITY – ROUTINES THAT TRANSFORM LIVES

The Psychology of Habits – Motivation and Behavior

Habits, at their core, are a fascinating interplay of psychology and behavior. They are shaped by motivation—our internal drive to act—and solidified through repetition, eventually becoming automatic. Understanding the psychology of habits offers us insight into why some behaviors stick while others fizzle out, and, more importantly, how we can leverage this understanding to create routines that drive productivity and personal growth.

Motivation is often described as the spark that initiates action. However, contrary to popular belief, motivation alone is rarely enough to sustain a habit. While the initial burst of enthusiasm might compel someone to sign up for a gym membership or start journaling, it is the consistency of action that determines whether these behaviors become ingrained. This is where habits bridge the gap between fleeting motivation and lasting behavior. By automating actions, habits remove the need to rely on willpower, which is finite and prone to depletion.

The relationship between motivation and habits is well illustrated by the experiments of Russian physiologist Ivan Pavlov in the early 20th century. Pavlov's groundbreaking work on classical conditioning demonstrated how behavior could be influenced by external stimuli. In his famous experiment, Pavlov rang a bell each time he fed his dogs. Over time, the dogs began to associate the sound of the bell with food, salivating even when no food was present. This learned association—where an external cue triggers an automatic response—mirrors the way habits are formed. While humans are far more complex than Pavlov's dogs, the principle remains the same: cues in our environment can trigger habitual behaviors, whether it's the sound of an alarm signaling the start of a morning routine or the sight of a coffee mug prompting the habit of brewing a cup.

What sets human habits apart, however, is the role of identity. While Pavlov's dogs responded purely to external conditioning, humans possess the unique ability to align habits with their sense of self. James Clear, a prominent author on habit formation, describes identity as the ultimate driver of lasting change. He argues that the habits we sustain are those that reinforce who we believe we are — or aspire to be. For example, a person who identifies as a runner is far more likely to maintain the habit of jogging than someone who sees it as a temporary means to lose weight. The action aligns with their self-perception, creating a positive feedback loop where the behavior reinforces the identity, and the identity strengthens the behavior.

This connection between identity and habits is evident in the lives of historical figures who achieved extraordinary productivity. Consider the case of Vincent van Gogh, whose identity as an artist drove his relentless pursuit of creative expression. Despite numerous setbacks, including financial struggles and periods of mental illness, van Gogh maintained the habit of painting daily. For him, the act of creating wasn't just something he did — it was who he was. This alignment between his identity and his actions sustained him through adversity, resulting in a body of work that continues to inspire millions.

While identity plays a significant role in habit formation, it's important to acknowledge the influence of external factors. Our environment, for instance, can either support or hinder our ability to build productive routines. Behavioral psychologist B.J. Fogg emphasizes the importance of "designing for success," a concept that involves shaping our surroundings to make good habits easier and bad habits harder. For example, placing a journal on your bedside table acts as a visual cue to write each night, while keeping distractions—like a smartphone—out of reach reduces the likelihood of mindless scrolling. By creating an environment that aligns with your desired identity, you increase the likelihood of sustaining habits over the long term.

Motivation also interacts with habit formation through the concept of intrinsic and extrinsic rewards. Intrinsic rewards, such as the satisfaction of learning a new skill or the joy of completing a creative project, tend to foster longer-lasting habits than extrinsic rewards, like monetary incentives or social recognition. This is because intrinsic rewards align more closely with our internal values, making the habit feel inherently meaningful. For example, someone who starts meditating to feel calmer and more centered is more likely to stick with the practice than someone who does it solely to follow a trend.

To create lasting habits, it's essential to understand and harness these psychological dynamics. One practical approach is to start by defining
your identity in relation to your goals. Ask yourself, "Who do I want to become?" rather than
focusing solely on what you want to achieve. If
your goal is to write a book, frame it in terms
of identity: "I am a writer." This subtle shift
transforms the goal from an external target into
an integral part of your self-concept, making it
easier to sustain the habits necessary to achieve
it.

Another effective strategy is to leverage small
wins to build momentum. Each time you follow
through on a habit, no matter how small, you
reinforce your identity and strengthen your
motivation. For example, completing a single
push-up can serve as a gateway to a full workout, just as writing one sentence can lead to an
entire chapter. These small victories create a
sense of accomplishment, which fuels further
action and builds confidence in your ability to
maintain the habit.

The psychology of habits reveals that motivation

and behavior are not isolated forces but part of a dynamic interplay influenced by identity, environment, and rewards. By aligning habits with your sense of self, designing your surroundings for success, and celebrating small wins, you can create routines that not only enhance productivity but also reflect the person you aspire to become. In doing so, you harness the true power of habits—not just as tools for achieving goals but as expressions of who you are.

Neuroscience in Action – How the Brain Builds Habits

The creation of habits is one of the brain's most remarkable functions—a process that allows humans to automate behavior, conserve energy, and focus on higher-order thinking. This automation is no accident; it's the product of the brain's evolutionary design, rooted in mechanisms that transform repeated actions into lasting routines. Understanding how habits are built in the brain provides not only a scientific framework for change but also a profound appreciation for the adaptability and resilience of the human mind.

At the heart of habit formation lies a process called **neuroplasticity**, the brain's ability to re-organize itself by forming new neural connections. Each time an action is repeated, the brain strengthens the pathways associated with that behavior, making it easier to perform. Think of it as a trail being worn into the forest floor—initially faint and difficult to follow, but becoming clearer and smoother with each step. This principle applies to everything from learning a new skill to solidifying daily routines. With enough repetition, the neural pathway becomes so well-trodden that the action feels effortless, requiring little conscious thought.

The **basal ganglia**, a small but powerful structure located deep within the brain, plays a central role in this process. Often referred to as the brain's habit center, the basal ganglia is responsible for recognizing patterns and automating repetitive tasks. This is why habits can feel so automatic: once a behavior is delegated to the basal ganglia, the prefrontal cortex—the part of the brain responsible for decision-making—can focus on more complex problems. This efficiency is a hallmark of human evolution, allowing early humans to save mental energy for survival tasks while automating basic routines like gathering food or building shelter.

The efficiency of the brain's habit-building mechanisms is both a strength and a challenge. While neuroplasticity enables the creation of beneficial habits, it also allows unproductive or harmful routines to take hold. Breaking these patterns requires significant effort because the brain, in its quest for efficiency, resists change. However, this same neuroplasticity offers hope: just as the brain can create and reinforce unwanted behaviors, it can also unlearn them, replacing them with more constructive patterns.

One of the most illuminating historical examples of how habits shape productivity comes from **Marie Curie**, the pioneering physicist and chemist who became the first person to win Nobel Prizes in two different sciences. Curie's disciplined routines were legendary. Each day, she adhered to a strict schedule that prioritized her research while leaving time for reflection and rest. This consistency allowed her to tackle groundbreaking experiments despite the challenges of limited resources and the societal barriers she faced as a woman in science. Her ability to maintain focus and perseverance, even in the face of adversity, was a testament to the power of habitual routines to channel intellectual energy effectively.

Curie's approach highlights a critical aspect of habit formation: the importance of repetition. The brain thrives on consistency. When an action is repeated under similar circumstances, the neural pathways associated with that behavior become increasingly robust. This is why consistent routines, no matter how small, have an outsized impact over time. For Curie, the simple act of dedicating specific hours to uninterrupted research reinforced her commitment to her work, enabling her to make discoveries that would change the course of history.

Modern neuroscience underscores the value of repetition in hardwiring habits. Studies on skill acquisition have shown that the number of repetitions required to solidify a behavior depends on its complexity. Simple habits, like drinking a glass of water after waking up, may take only a few weeks to form, while more complex routines, such as learning a new language or mastering an instrument, require sustained effort over months or even years. However, the principle remains the same: repetition creates familiarity, and familiarity breeds automation.

For individuals seeking to build productive habits, the lesson is clear: start small and repeat consistently. The brain responds best to manageable changes that can be reinforced over time. For example, if your goal is to establish a morning workout routine, begin with just five minutes of activity each day. While this may seem insignificant, it serves as the foundation upon which more substantial habits can be built. Over time, as the neural pathways strengthen, the habit will feel natural, paving the way for longer and more intense workouts.

Another fascinating insight from neuroscience is the role of **context** in habit formation. The brain is highly sensitive to environmental cues, which act as triggers for habitual behaviors. By associating a specific environment with a particular habit, you can create powerful mental connections that make the habit easier to sustain. For instance, dedicating a specific corner of your home to writing or meditating reinforces the brain's association between that space and the activity, increasing the likelihood of consistency.

The story of **Thomas Edison** further illustrates the interplay between repetition, context, and productivity. Edison, whose innovations shaped the modern world, famously maintained a consistent work environment that was carefully tailored to his needs. His laboratory served as a physical and mental anchor, a space where creativity and experimentation flourished. Edison's relentless repetition of experiments—often numbering in the thousands—was guided by the principle that breakthroughs emerge from persistence. This mindset, combined with his ability to create an environment conducive to focus, exemplifies how neuroscience and habit formation converge to drive extraordinary results.

The adaptability of the brain is a source of hope and empowerment. It reminds us that no matter how ingrained a habit may feel, change is always possible. By understanding how the brain builds habits—through repetition, environmental cues, and neuroplasticity—we gain the tools to design routines that align with our goals and values. This knowledge allows us to approach habit formation with patience and intentionality, recognizing that even the smallest actions, when repeated consistently, have the potential to shape our lives in profound ways.

Ultimately, the neuroscience of habits is a testament to the resilience and creativity of the human mind. By leveraging these principles, we can harness the brain's natural ability to adapt, transforming not only our routines but also our capacity to achieve greatness. Whether we draw inspiration from the disciplined routines of historical figures like Marie Curie or apply modern insights to our own lives, the science of habit formation offers a powerful blueprint for success.

The Habit Hierarchy – Prioritizing for Maximum Impact

Not all habits are created equal. While every action we repeat holds the potential to influence our lives, some habits exert a far greater impact than others. Understanding this distinction is critical for anyone striving to enhance productivity and achieve meaningful goals. By focusing on high-leverage habits—those with the power to create a cascade of positive effects across multiple areas of life—we can prioritize our efforts and maximize our growth.

The concept of a "habit hierarchy" provides a framework for distinguishing between habits that deliver exponential benefits and those that are merely superficial. At the top of this hierarchy are what are often called **keystone habits**: foundational routines that trigger a chain reaction of improvement. Keystone habits have a unique power to influence other behaviors, amplifying their impact and creating synergy across different domains of life. By contrast, superficial habits may offer some benefits but lack the transformative potential of their keystone counterparts.

Consider the daily routines of **Charles Darwin**, one of history's most influential scientists. Darwin's work reshaped our understanding of the natural world, but his achievements were not solely the result of innate genius. They were the product of deliberate, high-leverage habits. Each day, Darwin adhered to a disciplined schedule that balanced intense periods of focused study with time for relaxation and reflection. His mornings were dedicated to writing and research, a keystone habit that fueled his scientific discoveries. This routine didn't just advance his work; it also reinforced his mental clarity and emotional resilience, enabling him to maintain productivity over decades. Darwin's life illustrates how prioritizing keystone habits can amplify results far beyond the initial effort.

To identify high-leverage habits, it's essential to ask: **What actions provide the greatest return on investment?** These habits are often those that align most closely with our core values and goals. For instance, if health is a priority, regular exercise may be a keystone habit that not only improves physical fitness but also enhances mental focus, reduces stress, and boosts energy levels. Similarly, journaling can serve as a keystone habit for individuals seeking personal growth, fostering self-awareness, and clarifying intentions while encouraging other positive behaviors.

By contrast, superficial habits—though they may feel productive—often fail to deliver meaningful results. These are the routines that fill our time without advancing our goals, such as organizing digital files endlessly or checking email obsessively. While these actions may create a sense of accomplishment, they often serve as distractions from more impactful work. Recognizing the difference between high-leverage and superficial habits allows us to focus our energy where it matters most.

A helpful tool for prioritizing habits is the **Pareto Principle**, also known as the 80/20 rule. This principle suggests that 80% of results often stem from just 20% of efforts. Applied to habit formation, the Pareto Principle encourages us to identify the small number of habits that yield the most significant outcomes. For example, a writer might find that dedicating the first hour of each day to drafting new content (a keystone habit) produces the majority of their creative output, while less impactful tasks like formatting documents can be minimized or delegated. By concentrating on the high-leverage 20%, we can achieve disproportionate gains.

The ability to prioritize habits is not merely a matter of productivity; it's also a form of self-mastery. As individuals, we face an overwhelming array of choices every day. Without a clear framework for decision-making, we risk succumbing to the tyranny of the urgent—reacting to immediate demands rather than pursuing long-term objectives. The habit hierarchy serves as a compass, guiding us toward the actions that align with our values and aspirations.

The story of **Stephen R. Covey**, author of *The 7 Habits of Highly Effective People*, underscores the transformative power of prioritization. Covey's work popularized the idea of focusing on "big rocks"—the most important tasks that drive progress—while letting go of less significant activities. This principle applies equally to habits. By identifying and prioritizing the "big rocks" in our routines, we ensure that our daily actions contribute meaningfully to our overarching goals.

To implement the habit hierarchy in your own life, begin by reflecting on your aspirations. What are the outcomes you value most, and which habits have the greatest potential to support those outcomes? Once you've identified your high-leverage habits, commit to integrating them into your daily routine. Recognize that this process may require sacrifices, as focusing on impactful habits often means letting go of less meaningful activities. However, the rewards of this intentionality far outweigh the costs.

It's also worth noting that the habit hierarchy is not static. As our goals and circumstances evolve, so too should our habits. Periodic reflection allows us to reassess which routines remain high-leverage and which have become less relevant. This adaptability ensures that our habits continue to serve us as we grow and change.

Ultimately, the habit hierarchy is a tool for alignment. By prioritizing high-leverage habits, we bring our actions into harmony with our values, creating a sense of purpose and direction. Whether we draw inspiration from the disciplined routines of Charles Darwin or the principles espoused by Stephen Covey, the lesson is clear: the key to transformation lies not in doing more but in doing what matters most. In this way, the habit hierarchy empowers us to channel our energy effectively, unlocking our potential to achieve extraordinary results.

Flow States – Unlocking Peak Productivity

There is a rare and extraordinary state of mind where time seems to melt away, distractions fade into the background, and a person becomes entirely absorbed in the task at hand. This state, known as **flow**, is the pinnacle of productivity and creativity. It is the result of an alignment between challenge and skill, where the individual is neither bored nor overwhelmed but fully immersed in a sense of purpose and control. Understanding how to cultivate flow—and its connection to habits—is a gateway to unlocking human potential.

The concept of flow was first articulated by psychologist Mihaly Csikszentmihalyi, who spent decades studying this optimal state of performance. He observed that people across disciplines, from artists to athletes, described their most fulfilling and productive moments as those in which they were "in the zone." During flow, individuals experience heightened focus, creativity, and efficiency, often achieving results far beyond what seems possible in ordinary states of mind.

Flow is not an accidental phenomenon; it is closely linked to habits and routines. A key aspect of achieving flow is creating the right conditions—mentally, emotionally, and physically. Habits play a vital role in preparing the mind and body for this state. Regular routines, such as starting work at the same time each day or engaging in a consistent warm-up ritual, signal to the brain that it's time to focus. These habits reduce decision fatigue, freeing cognitive resources for deep engagement.

Few historical figures exemplify the mastery of flow as well as **Leonardo da Vinci**. Da Vinci's legendary creative output, from his meticulous scientific studies to his iconic works of art, was fueled by his ability to achieve deep focus. Despite his wide-ranging interests, da Vinci cultivated habits that allowed him to immerse himself fully in his work. For instance, he often engaged in deliberate periods of observation and sketching, which primed his mind for innovation. His notebooks reveal a man deeply engrossed in his craft, capturing ideas with precision and clarity. Da Vinci's life demonstrates that flow is not a product of chaos or sporadic inspiration but of intentional habits that create the conditions for brilliance.

Modern neuroscience sheds light on the mechanisms underlying flow. During this state, the brain enters a phase of **transient hypofrontality**, where activity in the prefrontal cortex — the area responsible for self-criticism and time awareness — decreases. This allows for greater creativity and a sense of timelessness. Additionally, the release of neurochemicals such as dopamine and norepinephrine enhances focus and motivation, making tasks feel more rewarding. The brain's natural reward system is thus activated, reinforcing the behaviors that lead to flow.

To cultivate flow, it's essential to design habits that align with its prerequisites. One of the most critical factors is balancing **challenge and skill**. Tasks that are too easy lead to boredom, while those that are overly difficult result in frustration. Flow emerges when the level of challenge is just right — demanding enough to require full attention but not so daunting as to feel insurmountable. Developing habits that gradually increase skill over time ensures that challenges remain engaging, paving the way for deeper immersion.

Another crucial element is **minimizing distractions**, a feat that requires deliberate habit formation in today's hyperconnected world. Setting boundaries around technology use, such as silencing notifications or creating tech-free zones, can help safeguard focus. For example, writers like Maya Angelou adopted routines to protect their creative flow. Angelou often rented a hotel room free of distractions to immerse herself in writing, bringing only the tools she needed for her craft. Her disciplined approach underscores the importance of creating an environment conducive to deep work.

Actionable habits can also include **priming rituals**—small, intentional actions that signal the brain to transition into a state of focus. Athletes, for example, often rely on warm-up routines to prepare mentally and physically for competition. These rituals, whether it's stretching, visualization, or listening to specific music, serve as cues that initiate flow. Similarly, professionals might start their workday with a brief review of goals or a moment of mindfulness to center their attention.

Flow states are not limited to solitary pursuits; they can also occur in collaborative settings, where shared habits and rhythms create synergy. In these contexts, trust and communication act as catalysts for flow, enabling teams to operate seamlessly. For instance, the improvisational performances of jazz musicians exemplify group flow, where individual mastery and collective harmony combine to produce something greater than the sum of its parts. These moments arise from shared habits of practice, listening, and responsiveness, demonstrating the universality of flow across disciplines.

The benefits of flow extend far beyond the immediate task at hand. Research shows that individuals who regularly experience flow report higher levels of satisfaction and well-being. This is because flow is intrinsically rewarding; it provides a sense of accomplishment and purpose that transcends external validation. By cultivating habits that promote flow, individuals not only enhance their productivity but also deepen their engagement with life.

To design habits that enable flow, it's helpful to

reflect on the conditions that foster your most focused and fulfilling moments. What environments, times of day, or types of activities bring out your best work? Start by incorporating small, consistent practices that align with these conditions. For example, if you notice that you achieve flow most easily in the morning, create a habit of reserving that time for your most important work. Over time, these habits will strengthen the neural pathways associated with flow, making it easier to access this state.

Flow is the intersection of discipline and inspiration, a state where habits and creativity converge to unlock human potential. By studying the routines of figures like Leonardo da Vinci and applying modern insights from neuroscience, we can learn to cultivate this powerful state in our own lives. Whether through deliberate priming rituals, minimizing distractions, or balancing challenge and skill, the path to flow is paved with intentional habits that prepare the mind and body for peak performance.

Ultimately, flow is more than a productivity tool; it is a way of being fully present, immersed in the pursuit of excellence. By unlocking this state, we transcend the mundane and step into a realm of possibility, where the ordinary becomes extraordinary and the boundaries of what we can achieve expand. The science of flow reminds us that greatness is not a fleeting moment of inspiration but the result of consistent habits that allow us to engage deeply with the world and our craft.

CHAPTER 3:
THE MORNING POWERHOUSE – STARTING THE DAY LIKE HISTORY'S GREATS

The Case for Mornings – How They Set the Tone

The morning is often referred to as the most important part of the day—a sacred window of opportunity to set the tone for everything that follows. Whether you're an artist, entrepreneur, or leader, the way you start your day carries a profound influence on your mindset, productivity, and success. Mornings are not just a time to get ready for the demands ahead; they are a chance to claim control over your life and begin with intention.

Science backs up this assertion. Studies show that willpower, much like a muscle, is strongest in the early hours of the day. As the day progresses, decision fatigue—a phenomenon where the quality of our choices deteriorates due to mental exhaustion—sets in. By tackling important tasks and establishing positive habits in the morning, we leverage this peak in willpower to our advantage. This is why many successful individuals prioritize their mornings, using this precious time to align their actions with their long-term goals.

Take, for instance, **Maya Angelou**, one of the most celebrated poets and authors of the 20th century. Angelou's mornings were deliberate and disciplined, reflecting her deep commitment to her craft. She often rented a hotel room in her city, free from distractions, where she would arrive early in the morning to write. Her routine was consistent: she worked for several hours, surrounded by nothing but a bed, a Bible, a dictionary, and a bottle of sherry. By dedicating her mornings to focused, uninterrupted work, Angelou harnessed the quiet clarity of the early hours to create some of the most iconic works in modern literature. Her example demonstrates how a structured morning routine can become a powerful driver of creativity and achievement.

Similarly, **Winston Churchill**, the British Prime Minister who led his nation through World War II, was known for his distinctive morning routine. Churchill began his day in bed, dictating correspondence, reading newspapers, and reviewing reports—all while enjoying a substantial breakfast. While unconventional, this routine allowed him to ease into his responsibilities and mentally prepare for the challenges of leadership. Churchill's mornings reflect an important truth: the "right" morning routine is not a one-size-fits-all formula but a deeply personal ritual that aligns with one's unique needs and goals.

The importance of mornings goes beyond individual success; they hold significant psychological power. How we begin our day often influences our mood, energy levels, and perception of challenges. A rushed or chaotic morning can lead to stress and anxiety, while a calm and intentional start fosters focus and confidence. This psychological principle is rooted in the idea of **priming,** where the initial moments of an experience shape how we interpret and respond to subsequent events. By crafting a purposeful morning routine, we "prime" ourselves for a day of productivity and resilience.

Modern neuroscience further supports the case for mindful mornings. The brain's **prefrontal cortex**, responsible for decision-making, planning, and self-control, is most active in the morning after a good night's sleep. This is the optimal time to engage in activities that require focus and strategic thinking, whether it's planning the day, tackling creative work, or solving complex

problems. Conversely, engaging in reactive behaviors—such as immediately checking emails
or scrolling through social media—can hijack
this productive state, setting a distracted tone
for the rest of the day.

To maximize the benefits of mornings, it's helpful to approach them with a mindset of intention
rather than obligation. Instead of viewing mornings as a race to catch up with the demands of
the world, we can treat them as an opportunity
to invest in ourselves. This shift in perspective
transforms the morning from a period of drudg-
ery to a source of empowerment.

The principles of an effective morning routine
are evident across history and disciplines. Beyond Angelou and Churchill, countless other
figures have credited their success to how they
spent their mornings. **Benjamin Franklin**, for
instance, began his day by asking himself a simple but profound question: "What good shall
I do this day?" This practice of reflection and
goal-setting grounded Franklin's mornings in
purpose, ensuring that his actions aligned with
his broader values. His routine serves as a reminder that even a few minutes of intentional

thought can have a transformative impact.

For today's readers, the lesson is clear: mornings are a powerful tool for shaping the trajectory of our lives. Whether you aspire to write a novel, lead a team, or simply navigate your day with greater clarity, the first hours of the morning offer a unique window of opportunity. Crafting a routine that reflects your priorities and values allows you to seize this opportunity and set a positive tone for the day ahead.

A well-designed morning routine doesn't have to be elaborate. In fact, simplicity often leads to greater consistency. The key is to focus on actions that bring clarity, energy, and alignment to your day. This might mean dedicating ten minutes to meditation, jotting down three key tasks for the day, or enjoying a quiet cup of coffee while reflecting on your goals. Whatever your approach, the act of starting your day with purpose creates a ripple effect that extends far beyond the morning hours.

In a world filled with distractions and demands, mornings offer a chance to reclaim control. They are a reminder that, no matter how unpredictable the rest of the day may be, the first moments belong to us. By investing in a thoughtful morning routine, we set ourselves up for success—not just in the tasks we accomplish but in the mindset we carry forward. The case for mornings is not simply about productivity; it's about living with intention, cultivating resilience, and beginning each day as the best version of ourselves.

Designing the Ideal Morning – A Blueprint for Success

Crafting the perfect morning routine is an art as much as it is a science. While there's no universal formula for success, an ideal morning routine is one that aligns with your personal values, goals, and natural rhythms. It's a blueprint that helps you transition smoothly from the tranquility of sleep to the demands of the day, laying a foundation of clarity, energy, and focus. The key is to create a routine that feels intentional yet adaptable—rigorous enough to provide structure but flexible enough to evolve with your needs.

One of the most intriguing examples of a methodical and highly personalized morning routine comes from **Nikola Tesla,** the visionary inventor. Tesla's mornings were marked by a profound sense of discipline and purpose. Rising early, he began his day with physical exercise, followed by a meticulous period of thought and planning. Tesla believed that the quiet hours of the morning were ideal for mental clarity and creative insight, often using this time to visualize his inventions in extraordinary detail. His ability to approach his work with such precision was not the result of chance but of a carefully cultivated routine that harnessed the unique power of mornings.

For Tesla, as for many others, the morning was not just a time to prepare for the day—it was a space for innovation and mastery. His routine serves as a reminder that the ideal morning is not about mimicking others' habits but about discovering what works best for you. With this in mind, let's explore the key principles of designing a personalized morning routine.

Step One: Start with Intention

The foundation of an effective morning routine

lies in clarity. Before building your routine, take time to reflect on your goals and priorities. Ask yourself: What outcomes do I want to achieve in the first hours of my day? Whether it's cultivating creativity, improving physical health, or simply creating a sense of calm, your intentions will serve as a compass for your actions.

For example, if your primary goal is to boost productivity, you might dedicate your mornings to focused work on high-priority tasks. On the other hand, if personal growth is your focus, you could prioritize activities like reading, journaling, or meditation. Tesla's mornings revolved around clarity and creation because those values aligned with his larger vision as an innovator. Similarly, your routine should reflect what matters most to you.

Step Two: Build Gradually

A common mistake when designing a morning routine is trying to overhaul your habits overnight. Lasting change is achieved through incremental adjustments rather than drastic shifts. Start with a single habit that resonates with your goals—whether it's waking up 15 minutes earlier, stretching for five minutes, or writing a single sentence in a journal—and build from there. These small, manageable changes create a sense of momentum, making it easier to incorporate additional habits over time.

Consider the story of **Benjamin Franklin**, who famously tracked his progress in living by 13 virtues. Franklin didn't attempt to perfect all virtues simultaneously; instead, he focused on one at a time, gradually incorporating each into his daily routine. This step-by-step approach can be applied to morning habits as well. By focusing on one habit at a time, you create a strong foundation upon which more complex routines can be constructed.

Step Three: Prioritize Balance

While structure is essential, an overly rigid routine can become a source of stress rather than empowerment. Flexibility ensures that your routine remains sustainable and adaptable to life's inevitable fluctuations. For instance, if your ideal morning includes a workout but you wake up feeling unwell, allow yourself to adjust by replacing it with light stretching or meditation. The goal is not perfection but consistency.

Balance also means creating a routine that nurtures both mind and body. Tesla's mornings combined physical activity with mental focus, a principle echoed by many high achievers. Activities like exercise, hydration, and healthy eating provide the energy needed for peak performance, while reflective practices like journaling or goal-setting cultivate mental clarity. Striking this balance ensures that your routine addresses all aspects of well-being.

Step Four: Optimize Your Environment

Your surroundings play a crucial role in shaping your habits. By designing an environment that supports your morning routine, you reduce friction and increase the likelihood of success. For example, if you plan to journal each morning, keep your notebook and pen on your bedside table as a visual cue. If exercise is part of your routine, lay out your workout clothes the night before.

Tesla's workspace reflected his need for focus and precision. Similarly, your environment should align with your goals, whether that means creating a quiet space for meditation, setting up a standing desk for morning work, or placing a water bottle within easy reach to encourage hydration. Small adjustments to your surroundings can have a significant impact on your ability to maintain a consistent routine.

Step Five: Reflect and Adjust

Even the most well-designed routine requires periodic reflection and refinement. As your goals and circumstances evolve, so too should your morning habits. Set aside time each month to evaluate your routine: What's working? What's not? Are there new habits you'd like to incorporate or old ones that no longer serve you? This process of reflection ensures that your mornings remain dynamic and aligned with your current priorities.

The idea of continuous refinement is exemplified by **Marie Curie**, whose disciplined routines enabled her to balance groundbreaking research with personal responsibilities. Curie regularly adapted her schedule to accommodate new experiments, demonstrating the importance of flexibility in sustaining long-term success. Her example reminds us that an ideal morning routine is not a static blueprint but a living framework that grows with us.

Conclusion

Designing the ideal morning is an opportunity to take ownership of your day and, by extension, your life. It's a chance to align your actions with your values, create space for growth, and set the tone for success. By starting with intention, building gradually, prioritizing balance, optimizing your environment, and embracing reflection, you can craft a routine that empowers you to thrive.

Whether your mornings resemble Tesla's disciplined starts or Franklin's reflective inquiries, the ultimate goal is the same: to begin each day with purpose and clarity. In a world where so much is beyond our control, the morning remains a precious space where we can choose how to show up—not just for the day ahead, but for ourselves.

The Role of Reflection – Mental Habits for Clarity

Amid the hustle and bustle of modern life, mornings offer a rare and precious opportunity to pause, reflect, and ground oneself. Reflection is not just an act of looking back; it's a deliberate practice of engaging with our thoughts, intentions, and emotions to gain clarity and purpose. By incorporating reflection into a morning routine, we cultivate a mental space that fosters mindfulness, self-awareness, and alignment with our values.

One of the most enduring examples of the power of reflection comes from **Marcus Aurelius**, the Roman emperor and philosopher. His meditative writings, later compiled into the work known as *Meditations*, reveal a man deeply committed to the practice of introspection. Each morning, Marcus Aurelius would take time to reflect on his duties, his principles, and the challenges he might face. He viewed this practice as a way to fortify his mind against distractions and temptations, ensuring that his actions were guided by wisdom rather than impulse. His reflections were not abstract musings but practical exercises that helped him navigate the complexities of leadership with resilience and grace.

For Marcus Aurelius, reflection was more than a habit—it was a cornerstone of his philosophy. He believed that by examining one's thoughts and actions, one could achieve a state of inner tranquility, unaffected by external chaos. This principle remains just as relevant today, offering a powerful tool for cultivating mental clarity in an increasingly noisy world.

Modern research supports the benefits of reflective practices like journaling and mindfulness. Studies show that journaling can improve emotional regulation, enhance problem-solving skills, and increase overall well-being. By putting thoughts onto paper, we externalize our inner dialogue, making it easier to identify patterns, clarify goals, and release anxieties. Similarly, mindfulness practices such as meditation help quiet the mind, reduce stress, and improve focus, creating a mental environment conducive to clarity and creativity.

Integrating these practices into a morning routine doesn't require hours of commitment. Even a few minutes of reflection can have a profound impact on the day ahead. For instance, starting the morning with a simple mindfulness exercise—such as focusing on your breath or observing your thoughts without judgment—can help center your attention and cultivate a sense of presence. This practice creates a mental reset, allowing you to approach the day with a calm and focused mindset.

Journaling, another powerful tool for reflection, offers a structured way to engage with your thoughts. One effective journaling exercise is the "three-question method," which involves answering the following prompts each morning:

1. What am I grateful for today?

2. What are my top priorities for the day?

3. What challenges might I face, and how can I prepare for them?

This practice mirrors the approach of Marcus Aurelius, who often reflected on similar questions in his writings. By starting the day with gratitude, intention, and foresight, journaling provides a roadmap for navigating the day with clarity and purpose.

Historical figures across disciplines have used reflection to fuel their achievements. Consider **Leonardo da Vinci**, whose journals are a testament to his insatiable curiosity and introspection. Da Vinci used his notebooks to sketch ideas, record observations, and pose questions about the world around him. This habit of documenting his thoughts not only preserved his insights but also sparked new connections, driving his innovations in art, science, and engineering. Da Vinci's example illustrates how reflection can unlock creativity and expand the horizons of what's possible.

For those new to reflective practices, the key is to start small and remain consistent. Reflection doesn't have to be elaborate; it can be as simple as pausing for a moment of gratitude or jotting down a single insight. The goal is not perfection but progress—a gradual deepening of self-awareness and intention. Over time, these small acts of reflection build a habit of mindfulness that permeates every aspect of life.

The practice of reflection also serves as a counterbalance to the reactive tendencies of modern life. In a world dominated by notifications, deadlines, and endless to-do lists, it's easy to become swept up in external demands. Reflection provides a moment of stillness—a chance to step back, recalibrate, and ensure that our actions align with our values. This deliberate pause not only enhances productivity but also fosters a sense of fulfillment, as we take ownership of our choices and focus on what truly matters.

To create a morning routine that incorporates reflection, consider designing a dedicated space for this practice. Whether it's a quiet corner of your home, a park bench, or even a comfortable chair by a window, having a designated area signals to your brain that it's time to slow down and reflect. Pairing this space with a cup of tea or a favorite journal can further enhance the ritual, making it a moment to look forward to each day.

Reflection is not just about looking inward; it's also about looking forward. By beginning each day with a moment of clarity, we set the stage for intentional action and meaningful progress. As Marcus Aurelius wrote, "When you arise in the morning, think of what a privilege it is to be alive—to think, to enjoy, to love." These words remind us that mornings are not just a time to prepare for the day but an opportunity to connect with our higher purpose.

Incorporating reflection into a morning routine transforms the start of the day into a powerful act of self-leadership. It enables us to face challenges with resilience, approach opportunities with focus, and navigate life's complexities with grace. Whether through mindfulness, journaling, or meditative practices, the role of reflection is clear: it is a compass that guides us toward clarity, purpose, and inner peace.

Energy and Momentum – Physical Habits That Drive Productivity

Mornings are not just a time for mental clarity and planning; they are also the perfect opportunity to energize the body and build momentum for the day ahead. Physical habits—like movement, hydration, and exposure to natural light—play a crucial role in setting the tone for productivity and well-being. These simple yet impactful actions create a foundation of vitality that supports both mental and physical performance throughout the day.

One of the most intriguing morning practices comes from **Benjamin Franklin**, who famously began his day with what he called an "air bath." Franklin would spend time each morning sitting in his room unclothed, allowing fresh air to wash over him while he reflected and planned his day. While unconventional by modern standards, Franklin's practice highlights the importance of intentional routines that awaken the body and mind. His "air bath" was not just a moment of relaxation but a deliberate act to energize himself for the challenges of the day. It serves as a reminder that small, consistent habits can have profound effects on our overall sense of vitality.

Physical activity is perhaps the most transformative morning habit. Exercise, even in small amounts, boosts circulation, increases oxygen flow to the brain, and releases endorphins— chemicals that elevate mood and reduce stress. Whether it's a brisk walk, a short yoga session, or a full workout, movement in the morning kickstarts the body's metabolism and primes the mind for focus and creativity. Studies have shown that people who engage in morning exercise tend to experience higher levels of productivity, better decision-making, and improved emotional resilience.

The story of **Theodore Roosevelt** illustrates the power of morning exercise in building energy and momentum. Roosevelt, known for his boundless energy and robust leadership, often began his day with intense physical activity, such as hiking, boxing, or horseback riding. For Roosevelt, exercise was more than a physical routine—it was a way to cultivate discipline, sharpen his mind, and prepare for the demands of his role as president. His commitment to physical vigor reflects the profound connection between movement and productivity.

Another cornerstone of morning energy is **hydration**. After a night of sleep, the body is naturally dehydrated, which can lead to feelings of sluggishness and reduced cognitive function. Replenishing fluids first thing in the morning helps jumpstart the body's systems, improving energy levels and mental clarity. A glass of water upon waking is a simple yet powerful habit that lays the foundation for a productive day.

In addition to hydration, **nutrition** plays a pivotal role in sustaining energy throughout the morning. A balanced breakfast that includes protein, healthy fats, and complex carbohydrates provides the fuel needed for sustained focus and performance. Avoiding heavy, sugary foods prevents energy crashes later in the day, ensuring that the morning momentum carries forward.

One often overlooked but highly effective morning habit is **exposure to sunlight**. Natural light regulates the body's circadian rhythm, the internal clock that governs sleep-wake cycles and energy levels. Morning sunlight exposure triggers the release of serotonin, a hormone that enhances mood and focus while setting the stage for restful sleep at night. Spending even a few minutes outdoors or near a bright window can have a significant impact on mental and physical well-being.

The importance of sunlight in the morning is supported by the practices of **Mahatma Gandhi**, who often began his day with a walk in the early morning light. These walks were not only a form of physical exercise but also an opportunity to connect with nature and reflect on his mission. Gandhi's simple yet profound habit illustrates how exposure to natural elements can enhance both energy and purpose, fostering a sense of connection and clarity that extends throughout the day.

For those looking to incorporate physical habits into their morning routines, the key is to start with small, achievable actions. Begin with a single glass of water upon waking, a brief stretch, or a walk around the block. These modest habits, when practiced consistently, create a ripple effect that improves overall energy and momentum. Over time, they can evolve into a more comprehensive routine that aligns with individual goals and preferences.

It's important to remember that physical habits are not just about enhancing productivity—they are also acts of self-care. By prioritizing the body's needs in the morning, we send a powerful message to ourselves: that our well-being matters, and that we are worth investing in. This mindset of care and intention creates a positive feedback loop, where physical vitality supports mental clarity, and vice versa.

The mornings of historical figures like Franklin, Roosevelt, and Gandhi demonstrate the transformative potential of physical habits. Their routines were not grand or elaborate; they were simple, intentional practices that energized their bodies and minds, enabling them to achieve extraordinary things. Their examples remind us that the path to greatness often begins with small, deliberate actions that build momentum and set the tone for the day.

Ultimately, physical habits in the morning are about more than just energizing the body—they are about creating a foundation of strength and resilience that carries forward into every aspect of life. Whether it's through movement, hydration, sunlight, or other practices, these habits empower us to approach the day with vitality and focus. By cultivating energy and momentum in the morning, we unlock the potential to live each day with purpose, clarity, and unwavering drive.

CHAPTER 4: THE KEYSTONE HABIT – UNLOCKING EXPONENTIAL GROWTH

What Are Keystone Habits? – The Levers of Change

In the complex web of human behavior, certain habits hold the power to transform not just individual routines but entire lives. These are **keystone habits**, the central pillars upon which broader changes are built. Unlike ordinary habits, keystone habits create a ripple effect, influencing other behaviors and fostering a sense of identity and purpose. They act as levers of change, requiring relatively small effort to yield significant results across multiple areas.

The concept of keystone habits gained prominence through the work of behavioral psychologists and was popularized by Charles Duhigg in *The Power of Habit*. According to Duhigg, keystone habits are unique because they trigger a chain reaction of improvements. When one key behavior shifts, it often reshapes attitudes, priorities, and routines, cascading into other aspects of life. For instance, adopting regular exercise as a keystone habit often leads to better eating choices, improved sleep, and increased productivity—changes that far exceed the original goal.

Keystone habits don't just change what we do; they shape who we are. They reinforce identity, helping us align our actions with the person we aspire to become. This profound impact sets them apart from habits that might provide isolated benefits but fail to create lasting, systemic change.

One of the most inspiring examples of a keystone habit in action comes from **Franklin D. Roosevelt**, the 32nd president of the United States. During the Great Depression, Roosevelt prioritized optimism—not just as a political stance but as a deliberate habit that influenced his daily actions and decisions. His "Fireside Chats," a series of radio broadcasts that addressed the American people, were a direct extension of this habit. Roosevelt's optimistic tone and reassuring words weren't incidental; they were cultivated through his consistent focus on instilling hope in himself and others.

This habit of optimism extended far beyond his speeches. It shaped his interactions with advisors, his policies, and even his demeanor in public appearances. As the nation grappled with unprecedented economic hardship, Roosevelt's keystone habit of optimism became a beacon of resilience, inspiring collective confidence and laying the groundwork for recovery. His example demonstrates that keystone habits aren't limited to personal growth—they can influence communities and even nations.

The ripple effect of keystone habits is further illustrated by the story of **Katharine Graham**, the publisher of *The Washington Post*. Faced with immense challenges, including taking over the company after her husband's death, Graham cultivated a keystone habit of deliberate preparation. Each morning, she meticulously reviewed briefings and sought advice from trusted mentors. This habit of preparation not only strengthened her leadership skills but also instilled a sense of confidence that allowed her to navigate the tumultuous publication of the Pentagon Papers. Graham's keystone habit of preparation became the foundation for her success, reinforcing other behaviors like decision-making, adaptability, and effective communication.

Keystone habits are powerful because they operate on multiple levels. On the surface, they drive immediate actions—like Roosevelt's daily reflections on optimism or Graham's disciplined preparation. But beneath the surface, they foster a mindset of growth and intentionality. This dual impact—shaping both behavior and identity—makes keystone habits particularly effective at catalyzing transformation.

Identifying a keystone habit often begins with examining areas of life that feel stuck or disconnected from larger goals. What small change could set off a positive chain reaction? For example, someone struggling with low energy might discover that consistent sleep patterns act as a keystone habit, improving their focus, mood, and physical health. Similarly, a professional aiming to enhance their productivity might find that a keystone habit of planning their day each morning unlocks greater efficiency and reduces stress.

Keystone habits are unique to each individual, shaped by personal values, aspirations, and circumstances. However, they share common characteristics: they create momentum, inspire other positive changes, and reinforce a sense of identity. This combination makes them incredibly impactful, often exceeding the scope of their original intent.

To harness the power of keystone habits, it's helpful to start small. Big changes can be intimidating, but a single, manageable habit can pave the way for exponential growth. For instance, the simple act of setting aside five minutes each morning to reflect on priorities can transform how the rest of the day unfolds. Over time, this small habit can expand into a broader routine of goal-setting, journaling, or mindfulness, creating a ripple effect of clarity and purpose.

It's also important to recognize that keystone habits don't operate in isolation—they thrive in supportive environments. Creating cues and rewards that reinforce the habit makes it more likely to stick. For example, if regular exercise is your keystone habit, laying out workout clothes the night before (cue) and treating yourself to a healthy smoothie afterward (reward) strengthens the behavior. These external reinforcements, combined with the intrinsic rewards of personal growth, amplify the habit's impact.

The potential of keystone habits lies not just in their ability to change individual lives but also in their capacity to inspire collective transformation. In organizations, keystone habits like fostering open communication or prioritizing employee well-being can create a culture of collaboration and innovation. In communities, habits like volunteering or promoting sustainability can spark movements that ripple outward, influencing policies and societal norms.

Ultimately, keystone habits are more than just routines—they are catalysts for growth, resilience, and alignment. They remind us that small, intentional actions can have far-reaching consequences, shaping not only what we do but who we become. By identifying and cultivating these powerful habits, we unlock the potential for transformation, one ripple at a time.

Historical Keystone Habits – Lessons from the Greats

History is rich with examples of individuals who achieved extraordinary things, not through chance but through the deliberate cultivation of keystone habits. These habits served as the foundation for their broader achievements, creating ripple effects that amplified their impact. By examining the lives of these figures, we can uncover valuable lessons on how keystone habits function as catalysts for growth and innovation, and how similar habits can be adapted to modern life.

One of the most striking examples of a keystone habit comes from **Thomas Edison**, the prolific inventor whose innovations shaped the modern world. Edison's ability to produce groundbreaking inventions, from the phonograph to the lightbulb, was underpinned by his strict adherence to daily schedules. He approached his work with unwavering discipline, dividing his time between experimentation, documentation, and reflection. This routine was not rigid for the sake of rigidity—it provided a structured framework that allowed him to focus his creative energies effectively.

Edison's keystone habit of maintaining a strict schedule had a cascading effect on his productivity. By dedicating specific hours to experimentation, he created a predictable rhythm that minimized distractions and maximized output.

This habit also reinforced his identity as an inventor, a role he embodied so fully that his life's work became synonymous with innovation itself. Edison's example illustrates how keystone habits can align daily actions with overarching goals, creating a sense of purpose that drives sustained effort.

The power of keystone habits is further exemplified by **Winston Churchill**, whose leadership during World War II hinged on a habit of deliberate preparation. Churchill's mornings often began with meticulous planning, reviewing reports, and crafting speeches that would inspire a nation. His habit of preparation extended beyond his personal routine; it became a cornerstone of his leadership style. Churchill's attention to detail ensured that he was always ready to respond to the challenges of war, whether in parliamentary debates or military strategy sessions.

Churchill's keystone habit of preparation also had a psychological ripple effect, instilling confidence not only in himself but also in those he led. His ability to articulate a clear vision, grounded in thorough preparation, rallied both soldiers and civilians, fostering unity and resilience. This habit exemplifies how keystone habits can transcend individual benefit, influencing the collective strength of a community or organization.

Another historical figure whose keystone habit shaped his success is **Mahatma Gandhi,** whose practice of daily prayer and reflection was integral to his leadership in India's struggle for independence. Gandhi's habit of setting aside time for introspection reinforced his commitment to nonviolence and truth, values that defined his movement. This daily ritual provided him with the clarity and resolve needed to lead a nation through turbulent times.

Gandhi's keystone habit of reflection was not merely a personal act; it became a source of inspiration for those around him. His example demonstrated that discipline and intentionality in small, consistent actions could influence broader societal change. Gandhi's habit serves as a reminder that keystone habits often align with deeply held values, creating a foundation of authenticity and integrity that inspires trust and followership.

Drawing parallels to modern life, it's evident that many of the habits cultivated by historical figures remain relevant today. For example, Edison's disciplined schedule finds its contemporary counterpart in time-blocking, a productivity technique used by professionals to allocate specific hours for focused work. Similarly, Churchill's emphasis on preparation resonates with the practice of daily goal-setting, which helps individuals prioritize tasks and maintain clarity amid competing demands.

The principle of keystone habits is not confined to extraordinary figures; it is accessible to anyone willing to embrace intentionality and consistency. Consider the story of **Serena Williams**, whose keystone habit of visualization has been a driving force behind her success as a tennis champion. Before every match, Williams spends time mentally rehearsing her performance, imagining every serve, volley, and point with precision. This habit not only sharpens her focus but also builds her confidence, enabling her to approach each match with a winning mindset. Williams' habit of visualization echoes the principles practiced by Gandhi, Edison, and

Churchill: small, deliberate actions that create a ripple effect of positive outcomes.

One of the most important lessons from these examples is that keystone habits are often deceptively simple. They don't require dramatic changes or grand gestures; instead, they involve small, consistent behaviors that align with larger goals. These habits gain their power from their ability to influence other aspects of life, creating a network of interconnected improvements. Whether it's Edison's scheduling, Churchill's preparation, Gandhi's reflection, or Williams' visualization, the common thread is intentionality.

For those seeking to adopt keystone habits in their own lives, the key is to identify behaviors that resonate with their values and goals. Keystone habits are deeply personal, and their impact is amplified when they are aligned with one's identity. For instance, a person striving to improve their health might adopt a keystone habit of preparing healthy meals, which can lead to better energy levels, improved focus, and enhanced overall well-being. Similarly, a professional aiming to advance their career might cultivate a habit of continuous learning, which can spark innovation, build confidence, and open new opportunities.

The lives of historical figures demonstrate that keystone habits are not about perfection but about progress. These habits create a framework for growth, enabling individuals to navigate challenges with resilience and purpose. They remind us that even the smallest actions, when performed with intention, can lead to extraordinary results.

By drawing inspiration from the keystone habits of the greats, we can begin to craft our own paths to growth and success. Whether it's through disciplined routines, deliberate preparation, or mindful reflection, the principles of keystone habits offer a timeless blueprint for unlocking exponential potential. Through small, intentional changes, we can create ripple effects that shape not only our own lives but also the world around us.

Choosing Your Keystone Habit – A Practical Guide

Keystone habits are powerful not because they address every challenge directly, but because they create a foundation for transformation. By identifying and cultivating just one of these habits, you can ignite a chain reaction of positive change across various aspects of your life. But how do you choose the right keystone habit? The process begins with understanding yourself—your goals, values, and the obstacles you face—and identifying the single behavior most likely to act as a catalyst for growth.

The first step in choosing a keystone habit is to reflect on what truly matters to you. Keystone habits are most effective when they align with your core values and long-term aspirations. Start by asking yourself: **What is the most significant area of my life I want to improve?** Whether it's your health, relationships, career, or personal growth, the answer will help narrow your focus. The keystone habit you choose should feel meaningful and connected to your identity, as this alignment creates the motivation needed to sustain it.

Consider the example of **Charles Darwin**, whose keystone habit of daily walks helped him achieve some of the most groundbreaking scientific insights of his time. For Darwin, these walks were more than a physical activity—they were a mental reset, a space to reflect on his theories and observations. By aligning this habit with his intellectual pursuits, Darwin ensured it contributed directly to his broader goals. His story highlights the importance of choosing habits that resonate deeply with your purpose.

Another way to identify a keystone habit is to look for behaviors that have a **multiplier effect**—actions that improve multiple areas of life simultaneously. For example, regular exercise is a classic keystone habit because it not only enhances physical health but also boosts mental clarity, emotional resilience, and self-confidence. Similarly, habits like journaling or daily planning can sharpen focus, reduce stress, and improve decision-making, creating benefits that extend far beyond the habit itself.

Once you've identified potential keystone habits, evaluate them using these three criteria:

1. **Impact**: Does this habit have the potential to create significant positive change in your life?

The more far-reaching the benefits, the more valuable the habit.

2. **Alignment**: Does this habit align with your values and long-term goals? Keystone habits are most effective when they reinforce your identity and aspirations.

3. **Simplicity**: Is this habit simple enough to implement consistently? Keystone habits don't have to be grand gestures—they often start with small, manageable actions that grow over time.

For those unsure of where to start, consider experimenting with simple yet impactful habits. For instance, beginning each day with a few minutes of mindfulness can set the tone for greater focus and intention. Similarly, a habit as straightforward as making your bed each morning can instill a sense of accomplishment and discipline, as noted by Admiral William H. McRaven in his famous commencement speech. These small victories build momentum, paving the way for more substantial changes.

Another effective strategy is to identify a **keystone behavior from your past**—a habit that previously brought significant benefits. Perhaps there was a time when regular exercise improved your energy levels, or when journaling helped you navigate a challenging period. Reflecting on these experiences can reveal clues about which habits resonate most strongly with your personality and needs.

For example, consider the story of **Oprah Winfrey**, whose keystone habit of gratitude journaling has been a cornerstone of her personal growth and success. By taking a few moments each day to reflect on what she's grateful for, Winfrey reinforces a mindset of abundance and positivity. This habit has not only influenced her emotional well-being but also shaped her approach to leadership and creativity. Winfrey's practice demonstrates how a single, well-chosen habit can amplify success across multiple dimensions.

To help you select your keystone habit, try this simple exercise:

1. Write down three areas of your life where you'd like to see improvement (e.g., health, relationships, career).

2. For each area, brainstorm three small actions that could create a positive ripple effect. For example:
- Health: Morning stretches, a daily walk, or drinking more water.
- Relationships: Sending a kind message to a loved one, practicing active listening, or scheduling regular quality time.
- Career: Setting daily goals, prioritizing tasks, or dedicating 15 minutes to professional reading.

3. Reflect on which of these actions feels most impactful and realistic to implement. The habit you choose should feel achievable yet meaningful.

Once you've chosen your keystone habit, the next step is to align it with your long-term goals. This alignment ensures that the habit doesn't exist in isolation but becomes a stepping stone toward broader aspirations. For example, if your goal is to write a book, your keystone habit might be dedicating 15 minutes each morning to freewriting. If your goal is to improve your health, your keystone habit could be preparing balanced meals in advance. By connecting the habit to a larger vision, you give it a sense of purpose that fuels consistency.

It's also helpful to visualize the ripple effects of your keystone habit. Imagine how a single change could influence other aspects of your life. For instance, adopting a habit of daily exercise might lead to better sleep, improved mood, and increased confidence, all of which enhance your ability to pursue personal and professional goals. This mental exercise reinforces the value of the habit, making it easier to stay committed.

Finally, remember that choosing a keystone habit is not about perfection—it's about progress. Start small, be patient with yourself, and allow the habit to grow naturally over time. As you witness its ripple effects, you'll gain the momentum and motivation needed to sustain it.

The process of selecting a keystone habit is deeply personal, but the principles remain universal: focus on what matters most, start with small, impactful actions, and align your habits with your values and goals. By following these steps, you can unlock the transformative power of keystone habits, creating a foundation for exponential growth in every area of your life.

Sustaining Keystone Habits – From Breakthroughs to Routine

The true power of a keystone habit lies not in its discovery but in its sustainability. While identifying and starting a transformative habit is a significant milestone, the real challenge is turning that habit into an enduring routine. Sustainability is the bridge between a fleeting breakthrough and long-term growth. It requires focus, accountability, and a deliberate approach to overcoming obstacles.

Keystone habits, by their nature, create a ripple effect, influencing other areas of life. However, their impact can diminish if they're not consistently practiced. The key to maintaining these habits is to embed them so deeply into daily life that they become second nature. To do this, we must understand the forces that sustain habits and learn to navigate the challenges that threaten their longevity.

The Role of Accountability

Accountability is one of the most effective strategies for sustaining keystone habits. When we hold ourselves accountable—whether through self-monitoring, external feedback, or shared goals—we reinforce the importance of the habit and its connection to our values.

Consider the story of **Mahatma Gandhi**, who not only practiced daily reflection as a keystone habit but also openly shared his principles with others. By aligning his personal habits with the collective goals of his movement, Gandhi created a sense of accountability that extended beyond himself. His commitment to reflection and nonviolence was not just a private discipline; it was a public pledge that inspired millions to hold him—and themselves—to higher standards.

For modern readers, accountability can take many forms. It might involve sharing your goals with a trusted friend or mentor, joining a community with similar aspirations, or using tools like habit-tracking apps. The key is to create a system of checks and balances that keeps you engaged and motivated.

Habit Tracking: Making Progress Visible

Tracking progress is a powerful way to sustain habits because it provides tangible evidence of growth. When you see the streak of days you've maintained a habit, it creates a sense of accomplishment and momentum. This visual reminder reinforces the behavior, making it more likely to stick.

Historical figures often used some form of tracking to sustain their keystone habits. **Benjamin Franklin**, for example, kept a daily journal in which he evaluated his adherence to 13 virtues he had identified as essential to self-improvement. By regularly assessing his progress, Franklin ensured that his habits remained at the forefront of his mind.

Today, habit tracking can be as simple as marking an "X" on a calendar or as sophisticated as using digital tools that provide data and insights. The act of recording progress serves as both a motivator and a diagnostic tool. If you notice a lapse in your habit, the data can help identify patterns and triggers, allowing you to adjust accordingly.

Overcoming Resistance and Setbacks

Even the most disciplined individuals encounter resistance and setbacks. Life's unpredictability can disrupt routines, leading to missed days or waning motivation. The key to sustaining a keystone habit is not to avoid setbacks entirely—an impossible task—but to recover quickly and learn from them.

When resistance arises, it's often rooted in competing priorities or internal doubts. To address this, it's helpful to revisit the **"why"** behind your keystone habit. Why did you choose this habit in the first place? What broader goals and values does it support? By reconnecting with your purpose, you can reignite the motivation needed to overcome resistance.

Setbacks, too, should be viewed as opportunities for growth rather than failures. The story of **Thomas Edison** offers a valuable perspective. Edison's experiments were often fraught with challenges and failures, yet he approached each setback with curiosity and determination. For

Edison, a failed experiment wasn't the end—it was a stepping stone to the next discovery. Similarly, a missed day or disrupted routine should be seen as a temporary detour, not a permanent derailment.

One practical strategy for overcoming setbacks is the **"never miss twice" rule**: if you miss a day, commit to resuming the habit the very next day. This approach prevents a single lapse from snowballing into a prolonged break. It reinforces the idea that consistency is more important than perfection.

The Power of Adaptation

Sustainability also requires flexibility. As life evolves, so too must your habits. A keystone habit that worked well in one phase of life may need to be adjusted to remain effective in another. For example, a new parent might need to modify their exercise routine to accommodate the demands of childcare, or a professional with a changing schedule might need to shift their morning routine to a different time of day.

Adapting a habit doesn't mean abandoning it;

it means finding ways to keep it relevant and aligned with your current circumstances. This adaptability ensures that the habit continues to serve its purpose without becoming a source of frustration or rigidity.

The example of **Marie Curie** illustrates the importance of adaptation. As her scientific career advanced, Curie adjusted her daily routines to balance her roles as a researcher, mother, and leader in the scientific community. Her ability to adapt her habits to her evolving responsibilities allowed her to sustain her productivity and impact over decades.

Creating a Supportive Environment

Environment plays a crucial role in sustaining habits. A well-designed environment reduces friction and makes it easier to maintain routines. For example, if your keystone habit is daily journaling, keeping your journal and pen in a visible, accessible location creates a cue that prompts the behavior. Similarly, if your habit is exercising in the morning, laying out your workout clothes the night before removes barriers to action.

A supportive environment also includes the people around you. Surrounding yourself with individuals who share your values and goals can create a culture of mutual encouragement. This social support not only reinforces your habit but also makes the journey more enjoyable.

The Long View: Building a Legacy

Sustaining a keystone habit is not just about short-term gains—it's about building a legacy of growth and resilience. Over time, the habit becomes an integral part of your identity, influencing how you approach challenges, pursue opportunities, and interact with the world.

The lives of historical figures like Gandhi, Franklin, and Curie remind us that sustaining a keystone habit is a journey, not a destination. It requires commitment, adaptability, and a willingness to learn from both successes and setbacks. By embracing these principles, you can transform a single habit into a cornerstone of lasting change.

Through accountability, habit tracking, and the

ability to adapt, your keystone habit becomes more than a routine—it becomes a source of strength and inspiration. It's the foundation upon which exponential growth is built, a daily reminder of your potential to achieve greatness. By sustaining your keystone habit, you unlock not only your own potential but also the power to inspire those around you, creating ripples of positive change that extend far beyond yourself.

CHAPTER 5: ADAPTING THROUGH CHAOS – RESILIENT HABITS IN TURBULENT TIMES

Habits as Anchors – Finding Stability Amid Uncertainty

In the midst of chaos, habits become the quiet anchors that provide stability and direction. When the world around us feels unpredictable, the routines we cultivate serve as constants, grounding us and preserving our mental clarity. They become more than mere actions; they are acts of resilience, creating structure amid uncertainty and helping us navigate turbulent times with a sense of purpose.

One of the most compelling examples of habits as anchors comes from **Nelson Mandela**, who endured 27 years of imprisonment under apartheid. Stripped of his freedom and subjected to dehumanizing conditions, Mandela relied on small, deliberate routines to maintain his dignity and resolve. Each day, he followed a schedule that included physical exercise, reading, and writing letters. These habits, though simple, gave him a sense of control over his circumstances. They reminded him that while he couldn't dictate his environment, he could govern his response to it.

Mandela's habit of daily exercise, for example, was a physical routine with profound psychological benefits. Running in place within the confines of his cell, he not only kept his body strong but also reinforced his mental discipline. Similarly, his habit of reading and writing allowed him to stay connected to the world beyond the prison walls, fueling his vision for a free and just South Africa. These routines were not acts of mere survival; they were acts of defiance, symbols of his refusal to let chaos dictate his identity.

The power of habits to provide stability lies in their predictability. When the external world is unpredictable, habits offer a sense of normalcy and rhythm. They reduce the cognitive load of decision-making, freeing mental energy for higher-order thinking and problem-solving. In chaotic situations, this clarity is invaluable. Habits act as a stabilizing force, enabling us to focus on what we can control rather than being consumed by what we cannot.

The role of habits as anchors is not limited to extraordinary circumstances like Mandela's imprisonment; it extends to the everyday turbulence that many people face. During times of personal upheaval—whether it's the loss of a job, a health crisis, or a period of intense change—habits create a framework for resilience. A morning cup of tea, a nightly walk, or a few minutes of journaling can serve as touchstones, reminding us of our capacity to find steadiness within ourselves.

Scientific research supports the idea that habits can protect mental clarity during periods of stress. Studies show that routines reduce anxiety by providing a sense of order and predictability. They also foster a sense of accomplishment, even in small measures, which boosts self-esteem and motivation. In this way, habits become a source of strength, helping us maintain a positive outlook even in challenging times.

For readers navigating their own uncertainties, the lesson is clear: lean into small, meaningful routines. You don't need grand gestures to anchor yourself; even the simplest habits can have a profound impact. Consider the practice of mindfulness, for instance. Taking just five minutes a day to focus on your breath or observe your thoughts without judgment can create a mental refuge amid chaos. This habit, though modest, trains the mind to stay present and calm, fostering resilience in the face of adversity.

The story of Nelson Mandela also highlights the importance of aligning habits with values. His routines weren't arbitrary; they reflected his commitment to strength, learning, and connection. By choosing habits that resonate with your core principles, you create routines that not only stabilize you but also reinforce your identity. For example, a habit of volunteering, even in small ways, can anchor a sense of purpose during times of uncertainty, reminding you of your capacity to contribute and make a difference.

It's worth noting that habits as anchors are not about denying the reality of chaos but about responding to it with intention. Chaos often brings with it a sense of powerlessness, a feeling that events are happening to us rather than being shaped by us. Habits disrupt this narrative. They shift the focus from what's beyond our control to what's within our grasp. In doing so, they transform chaos from a force of disruption into an opportunity for growth.

This principle is exemplified by another historical figure, **Victor Frankl**, a Holocaust survivor and psychiatrist. In his memoir *Man's Search for Meaning*, Frankl recounts how he and others in concentration camps found strength in small routines, such as sharing food or engaging in quiet acts of reflection. These habits, though seemingly inconsequential, helped preserve their humanity and gave them a sense of purpose. Frankl's insights underscore the profound psychological impact of habits as anchors, especially in the most extreme conditions.

For modern readers, the practical takeaway is to start small and stay consistent. Identify one or two habits that bring you a sense of calm or focus, and commit to practicing them regularly. These could be as simple as drinking a glass of water each morning, dedicating a few minutes to gratitude, or maintaining a consistent bedtime. The key is to choose habits that resonate with you personally, as their meaning amplifies their stabilizing effect.

As we navigate an increasingly fast-paced and uncertain world, the importance of habits as anchors cannot be overstated. They remind us that even in the midst of chaos, we have the power to create order and meaning. Like Mandela in his prison cell or Frankl in the camps, we can turn to small, deliberate actions to ground ourselves, preserve our clarity, and reaffirm our identity.

Habits are not just routines; they are acts of resilience and agency. They anchor us in the present while guiding us toward the future we wish to create. By cultivating habits that align with our values and goals, we build a foundation of stability that enables us to face uncertainty with courage and grace. In this way, habits become more than tools for survival—they become the building blocks of strength and transformation.

Lessons from Adversity – How the Greats Adapted

Adversity often brings out the most profound aspects of human resilience. Throughout history, individuals who faced extraordinary challenges have shown us that habits, when adapted creatively, can become tools for survival, innovation, and personal transformation. These stories not only inspire but also provide practical insights into how habits can be harnessed to navigate turbulent times.

One of the most powerful examples of adaptation through adversity is the life of **Helen Keller**, who overcame the dual barriers of blindness and deafness to become a renowned author, speaker, and activist. Keller's habits of relentless learning and communication were not innate but deliberately cultivated through her partnership with her teacher, Anne Sullivan. Sullivan taught Keller to connect with the world using tactile language—an approach that required both immense patience and discipline.

Keller's habit of continuous learning became her anchor. Each day, she practiced identifying objects through touch and forming associations with their names spelled into her hand. Over time, this habit transformed not only how she interacted with the world but also how she viewed herself. Keller's disciplined approach to learning expanded her sense of possibility, enabling her to transcend the limitations imposed by her disabilities. Her story exemplifies the principle that habits, when tailored to our circumstances, can unlock potential even in the face of overwhelming odds.

Like Keller, **Frida Kahlo**, the celebrated Mexican artist, turned to habits as a means of resilience and expression during a lifetime marked by physical pain and personal turmoil. Kahlo's habit of daily painting became both a refuge and a form of self-reinvention. Confined to her bed for extended periods due to a near-fatal bus accident, Kahlo transformed her physical limitations into a source of creative power. Using a mirror affixed above her bed, she painted self-portraits that explored themes of identity, suffering, and strength.

Kahlo's painting habit was not just a creative outlet—it was an act of defiance against her circumstances. By channeling her pain into art, she redefined her narrative, transforming chaos into beauty. Her story underscores the importance of finding habits that align with our passions and values, even in the most challenging times. For Kahlo, painting was not merely a routine but a lifeline, a way to assert control and give meaning to her experiences.

Both Keller and Kahlo demonstrate the adaptability of habits in the face of adversity. Their stories reveal a critical truth: resilient habits are not static. They evolve in response to changing circumstances, becoming tools of reinvention rather than rigid routines. This adaptability is a hallmark of resilient individuals, who view challenges not as insurmountable barriers but as opportunities to grow and innovate.

The principle of adaptability is further illustrated by the life of **Franklin Delano Roosevelt (FDR)**, who led the United States through the Great Depression and World War II while managing the debilitating effects of polio. After contracting the disease in his late 30s, Roosevelt initially struggled with despair and frustration. However, he eventually developed habits that helped him regain confidence and redefine his role as a leader.

One of Roosevelt's most notable habits was his commitment to swimming and physical therapy. These routines not only improved his physical strength but also symbolized his determination to overcome limitations. Moreover, Roosevelt adapted his public persona to emphasize his leadership qualities rather than his disability, focusing on habits that showcased his optimism, charisma, and strategic vision. His ability to adapt his routines and image allowed him to connect with the American people during one of the most tumultuous periods in history.

For contemporary readers, these stories offer valuable lessons on the role of habits in navigating adversity. First, they highlight the importance of aligning habits with personal strengths and passions. Keller's learning, Kahlo's painting, and Roosevelt's therapeutic routines were deeply connected to their identities and goals. These habits were not chosen arbitrarily — they were deliberate responses to their circumstances, designed to harness their unique abilities.

Second, these stories demonstrate the transformative power of flexibility. Resilient habits are not rigid; they adapt to the demands of the moment. This principle is particularly relevant in today's fast-changing world, where the ability to pivot and reinvent oneself has become a critical skill. By cultivating habits that are both intentional and adaptable, we can maintain a sense of agency even in the face of uncertainty.

Lastly, these examples underscore the value of habits as tools for innovation. Adversity often forces us to think differently and explore new approaches. Keller's tactile language, Kahlo's self-portraits, and Roosevelt's redefined leadership all emerged from the necessity of adapting to challenges. Their stories remind us that habits are not just routines—they are opportunities to experiment, create, and grow.

To apply these lessons in our own lives, we can start by identifying habits that align with our core values and circumstances. These habits don't need to be grand or complex; they can be as simple as journaling, practicing gratitude, or dedicating time to a creative pursuit. The key is to choose habits that resonate with who we are and where we want to go.

It's also helpful to approach adversity with a mindset of curiosity. Instead of viewing challenges as obstacles, we can see them as prompts for reinvention. What new habits could emerge from this situation? How can existing routines be adapted to meet new demands? By asking these questions, we open ourselves to the possibility of growth.

The lives of Helen Keller, Frida Kahlo, and
Franklin Roosevelt remind us that habits are
not just tools for navigating ordinary life—they
are lifelines during extraordinary times. Their
stories inspire us to view adversity not as a
limitation but as a catalyst for innovation and
resilience. By embracing habits that align with
our passions, adapting them to our circumstances, and using them as platforms for growth, we
can navigate even the most turbulent times with
strength and grace.

Building Resilient Habits – Tools for Tough Times

When life becomes turbulent, it's easy to feel
unmoored, as though the ground beneath us
has shifted. Yet, in the midst of chaos, resilient
habits can serve as both anchors and lifelines.
Unlike ordinary routines, resilient habits are
specifically designed to withstand challenges,
adapting to shifting circumstances while preserving a sense of stability and progress. By
cultivating these habits, we equip ourselves to
face adversity with strength and intention.

Resilient habits are built on a foundation of small, consistent actions that align with our core values and long-term goals. While the chaos of external circumstances can disrupt larger plans, these small habits offer a sense of control. A simple act, like taking a few deep breaths before a stressful meeting or setting aside time for reflection at the end of the day, can create a ripple effect, calming the mind and refocusing energy.

One effective approach to building resilient habits is **habit layering**. This technique involves attaching a new habit to an existing one, creating a seamless integration into daily life. For example, if you already have a habit of making coffee each morning, you might layer a mindfulness practice onto it, using the time it takes for the coffee to brew to focus on your breath or set an intention for the day. Habit layering works because it leverages the stability of established routines, making it easier to adopt new behaviors without overwhelming the mind.

The concept of habit layering can be traced back to the daily practices of figures like **Leonardo da Vinci,** whose structured habits allowed him to thrive in a chaotic world. Da Vinci's ability to balance artistic creativity with scientific inquiry was rooted in his methodical approach to work. By integrating habits of observation, note-taking, and experimentation into his daily routine, he built a framework that sustained his curiosity and productivity, even in the face of uncertainty. Da Vinci's story illustrates the power of layering habits that complement one another, creating a system of resilience that supports both consistency and innovation.

. Another tool for building resilient habits is the practice of **mindfulness**. Mindfulness trains the mind to stay present, reducing the tendency to become overwhelmed by uncertainty. This practice doesn't require elaborate rituals; even a few moments of focused awareness can make a significant difference. For instance, pausing to observe your surroundings during a walk or taking a mindful breath before responding to a challenging situation can cultivate clarity and calm. These small acts of mindfulness create a buffer against the stress of chaos, allowing us to approach difficulties with greater perspective.

Mindfulness was a cornerstone of **Buddhist philosophy**, but its principles have been embraced by leaders and thinkers across cultures and eras. Consider the example of **Marcus Aurelius**, the Roman emperor and Stoic philosopher. During his reign, Aurelius faced relentless challenges, from military conflicts to political intrigue. Yet, he maintained a habit of daily reflection, recording his thoughts and meditations in what would later become the book *Meditations*. This practice of mindfulness and self-examination helped him navigate the chaos of leadership with wisdom and composure. Like Aurelius, we can use mindfulness as a habit to ground . ourselves, even in the most turbulent times.

Building resilient habits also requires a sense of community and support. Adversity is rarely faced in isolation; our connections with others play a crucial role in sustaining us. Whether it's a circle of friends, a family network, or a professional community, these relationships provide encouragement, accountability, and shared strength. For instance, joining a group with similar goals—such as a fitness class, a book club, or a support group—can reinforce habits through collective effort.

The power of community in fostering resilience

is evident in the story of **Maya Angelou**, the acclaimed poet and activist. Throughout her life, Angelou drew strength from her relationships with mentors, colleagues, and friends. These connections supported her during periods of personal and professional upheaval, providing both inspiration and accountability. Her habit of engaging with a supportive community was not only a source of resilience but also a catalyst for her creative and social impact. Angelou's story reminds us that habits are not just individual practices; they are often shaped and strengthened by the people around us.

To build resilient habits in tough times, it's important to focus on flexibility rather than perfection. Life's challenges are rarely predictable, and rigid routines can become burdensome under pressure. Resilient habits are adaptive, capable of evolving in response to new circumstances. For example, if a daily exercise routine becomes impractical due to a change in schedule, it can be adjusted to a shorter workout or replaced with a different form of movement. The key is to preserve the essence of the habit—its purpose— while remaining open to modification.

The principle of flexibility is particularly relevant in the context of **habit stacking**, a strategy that involves linking small habits together to create a chain of positive behaviors. For instance, you might pair a gratitude practice with journaling, followed by a brief review of your goals for the day. This stack of habits creates a cohesive routine that can be easily adjusted as needed. If one part of the stack becomes challenging to maintain, the other elements can continue, preserving the overall momentum.

Resilient habits are also supported by clear goals and rewards. Setting specific, achievable objectives provides direction, while celebrating small victories reinforces the habit. For example, if your habit is to write 500 words a day, acknowledging each completed session with a reward—such as a favorite snack or a relaxing break—builds positive associations that strengthen the habit.

Ultimately, building resilient habits is about creating a toolkit for navigating life's challenges with grace and intention. These habits don't eliminate adversity, but they provide the stability, clarity, and strength needed to face it. By integrating strategies like habit layering, mind-fulness, community support, and adaptability, we can cultivate habits that endure, empower-ing us to thrive even in the toughest of times.

In a world that often feels uncertain, resilient habits remind us of our capacity to adapt, grow, and persevere. They are a testament to the power of small, deliberate actions to create ripples of positive change, not only in our own lives but also in the lives of those around us. Through these habits, we transform chaos into oppor-tunity, building a foundation of resilience that carries us forward.

Thriving Amid Change – Turning Chaos into Opportunity

Chaos often arrives uninvited, disrupting the familiar rhythms of life and leaving us searching for stability. Yet, history and human resilience repeatedly show us that upheaval, while chal-lenging, is also a fertile ground for transforma-tion. By shifting our perspective and leverag-ing habits, we can not only endure periods of change but also thrive within them, using chaos as a catalyst for growth and reinvention.

To see the potential for thriving amid change, we can look to history's great periods of upheaval, such as the **Renaissance**. Emerging from the turmoil of the Black Death and centuries of feudal stagnation, the Renaissance was a time of unprecedented creativity and discovery. Artists, scientists, and thinkers adapted to a world in flux, transforming adversity into opportunity. Figures like **Leonardo da Vinci** and **Galileo Galilei** developed habits of curiosity, experimentation, and relentless inquiry, driving advances that reshaped humanity's understanding of art, science, and the universe.

The Renaissance teaches us a profound lesson: change, while unsettling, clears the way for innovation. The disarray of the old order creates space for new ideas, new approaches, and new habits. For modern readers navigating their own periods of change, the Renaissance offers a reminder that chaos is not the end — it is a transition, an opportunity to reimagine what is possible.

To thrive during times of change, it's essential to cultivate habits that foster adaptability and creativity. One such habit is **reflection**, a practice embraced by Renaissance thinkers and equally valuable today. Reflection allows us to pause amid the whirlwind of change, to process what is happening, and to chart a course forward. This habit can take many forms, from journaling about daily experiences to meditating on long-term goals. Reflection creates a space for clarity, enabling us to see opportunities hidden within the chaos.

Consider the story of **Marie Curie**, who faced both personal and professional upheavals during her groundbreaking scientific career. After the death of her husband, Pierre, Curie could have succumbed to grief and the weight of her responsibilities. Instead, she adopted habits of reflection and focused work, immersing herself in research that would lead to the discovery of radium and polonium. Her ability to thrive in the face of adversity was rooted in her habits, which provided both a sense of stability and a channel for growth.

Another powerful strategy for thriving amid change is cultivating a mindset of **growth and experimentation**. When we view change as a series of opportunities rather than a string of losses, we unlock our potential for reinvention. Habits that encourage experimentation—such as trying new skills, engaging with diverse perspectives, or setting small, achievable challenges—foster a sense of agency. These habits allow us to explore new possibilities and adapt to shifting circumstances.

The example of **Thomas Edison** highlights the power of experimentation during times of uncertainty. Edison's invention of the lightbulb was not the result of a single stroke of genius but a process of relentless trial and error. He famously stated, "I have not failed. I've just found 10,000 ways that won't work." Edison's habit of approaching problems with curiosity and persistence enabled him to thrive amid the uncertainty of invention, turning setbacks into stepping stones.

In addition to reflection and experimentation, thriving amid change often requires a deliberate focus on **connection and collaboration**. Change can feel isolating, but habits that foster relationships—whether through mentoring, networking, or shared learning—create a sense of belonging and mutual support. Collaboration not only provides emotional resilience but also sparks creativity, as diverse perspectives lead to innovative solutions.

The Renaissance itself was a testament to the power of collaboration. Artists like Leonardo da Vinci and Michelangelo drew inspiration from scientists, philosophers, and patrons, creating works that reflected the collective genius of their time. Similarly, the habit of engaging with others during periods of change enriches our perspectives and amplifies our ability to adapt.

For modern readers, one practical way to foster connection is through intentional habits like regular check-ins with mentors or peers, joining communities aligned with personal or professional interests, or simply making time to strengthen personal relationships. These habits provide a network of support, reminding us that thriving amid change is not a solo endeavor—it is a shared journey.

While reflection, experimentation, and connection are powerful habits for thriving amid change, their effectiveness depends on one final ingredient: **resilience in action**. Thriving doesn't mean avoiding challenges—it means facing them with courage and a willingness to grow. Resilient habits, such as mindfulness, goal-setting, or prioritizing self-care, provide the foundation for sustained effort in the face of adversity.

The story of **Viktor Frankl**, a Holocaust survivor and psychiatrist, offers profound insights into the resilience needed to thrive amid chaos. In his memoir, *Man's Search for Meaning*, Frankl describes how he and others in concentration camps found strength through small, purposeful habits, such as sharing food, reflecting on loved ones, or finding humor in the bleakest moments. These habits didn't erase the horrors they faced, but they gave them the fortitude to endure and, ultimately, the capacity to rebuild their lives.

For readers seeking to thrive amid their own periods of change, Frankl's story underscores the importance of finding meaning in adversity. Habits that align with personal values and purpose create a sense of direction, even when external circumstances are uncertain. Whether it's dedicating time to a meaningful project, practicing gratitude, or helping others, these habits remind us of our ability to contribute and grow.

Ultimately, thriving amid change is not about returning to a past state of stability—it is about embracing the opportunities that chaos presents. By cultivating habits that encourage reflection, experimentation, connection, and resilience, we can transform periods of upheaval into chapters of growth. Like the Renaissance thinkers who emerged from the turmoil of their time, or the innovators and leaders who adapted to their own challenges, we too can use chaos as a canvas for reinvention.

In the face of change, habits become more than routines—they become acts of hope, courage, and creativity. Through these habits, we reclaim our agency, turning the uncertainty of the present into a foundation for the future. By viewing chaos not as a threat but as an opportunity, we unlock the potential to thrive, building a life that reflects both our resilience and our boundless capacity for growth.

CHAPTER 6: HABIT MASTERY – HOW TO BREAK BAD HABITS AND BUILD BETTER ONES

Understanding Bad Habits – Why They Stick

Habits are the silent architects of our lives, shaping our behaviors in ways we often don't recognize. While good habits propel us toward our goals, bad habits act as invisible barriers, pulling us into cycles of frustration and inertia. But why do these negative patterns persist, even when we know they're harmful? Understanding the psychology of bad habits and their triggers is the first step toward breaking free and regaining control.

At their core, bad habits are learned behaviors that serve a purpose, albeit often a misguided one. Psychologically, they are tied to the brain's reward system. When we engage in a particular action—whether it's procrastinating, overeating, or checking our phones excessively—it often provides a momentary sense of relief or pleasure. This reward reinforces the behavior, creating a loop that is difficult to break. Over time, the habit becomes automatic, embedded in the neural pathways of the brain.

One classic example of how bad habits form can

be seen in the early career of **Thomas Edison**, the prolific inventor. Before achieving success with the electric lightbulb, Edison encountered numerous failures, many of which were tied to his own habits. His tendency to overcommit to untested ideas and dive into projects without adequate planning often led to financial set-backs and wasted resources. For instance, his work on an automatic vote recorder—a device designed to speed up the legislative voting pro-cess—failed spectacularly because he didn't consider whether there was market demand for such a device. This habit of impulsivity hin-dered his progress until he learned to approach innovation with greater strategy and discipline.

Edison's story illustrates a critical point: bad habits are not moral failings or signs of weak-ness; they are patterns that can emerge in any-one's life. Recognizing this truth is liberating because it shifts the focus from judgment to self-awareness. To overcome bad habits, we must first understand what drives them.

One of the most powerful tools for understand-ing bad habits is **self-awareness**. This involves observing your behaviors objectively and identifying the triggers that set them into motion. Triggers can be external, such as specific environments or people, or internal, such as stress or boredom. For example, someone might notice that they reach for sugary snacks when feeling overwhelmed at work. The snack itself is not the root problem; it's the way the brain has learned to cope with stress by seeking comfort.

Developing self-awareness often requires asking reflective questions:

- When do I engage in this habit most frequently?

- What emotions or situations typically precede the behavior?

- What immediate benefit do I gain from the habit, and how does it affect me in the long term?

Through this process, patterns begin to emerge, revealing the underlying dynamics of the habit. For instance, if procrastination is a recurring issue, self-awareness might uncover a fear of failure as the trigger. Understanding this connection provides a foundation for addressing

the root cause rather than just the surface behavior.

Another important aspect of understanding bad
habits is recognizing their **cumulative impact**.
Individually, a bad habit might seem trivial—a
skipped workout here, a late-night binge-watch
there. But over time, these small choices add up,
shaping the trajectory of your life. This concept,
known as the **aggregation of marginal losses**,
highlights how seemingly minor behaviors can
lead to significant consequences when repeated
consistently.

Historical examples abound of individuals
who fell victim to bad habits, only to recognize
their impact and pivot toward change. **Winston
Churchill**, for instance, was known for his love
of rich foods and alcohol, habits that took a toll
on his health. However, during critical periods
of his leadership, he adapted by incorporating
healthier routines, such as taking long walks
and practicing moderation. Churchill's journey
underscores the importance of acknowledging bad habits without letting them define you.
Change is always possible, provided there is
a willingness to confront the patterns holding

you back.

For modern readers, understanding bad habits also involves grappling with the role of **technology**. In today's digital age, many habits—such as scrolling through social media or constantly checking notifications—are deliberately engineered to exploit the brain's reward system. Platforms are designed to capture attention and keep users engaged, creating habits that feel almost impossible to break. Recognizing this dynamic is crucial for regaining agency. Awareness of how these systems operate can empower individuals to set boundaries and reclaim their time.

Breaking free from bad habits begins with awareness but requires action. A useful framework for this process is the **habit loop model**, introduced by Charles Duhigg in his book *The Power of Habit*. According to this model, every habit consists of three components:

1. **Cue**: The trigger that initiates the habit.

2. **Routine**: The behavior itself.

3. **Reward**: The benefit gained from the behavior.

To disrupt a bad habit, it's essential to identify its cue and reward. For example, if the habit is staying up late watching TV, the cue might be the feeling of fatigue at the end of the day, and the reward might be the desire to unwind. By identifying these components, you can begin to experiment with alternative routines that satisfy the same reward. In this case, replacing TV time with reading or a relaxing bedtime ritual could serve as a more constructive way to unwind.

Self-awareness tools, such as journaling or tracking habits, can help illuminate these patterns. Writing down the times and circumstances of a bad habit creates a record that reveals its frequency and triggers. This data provides the clarity needed to design a plan for change.

Ultimately, understanding bad habits is not about perfection—it's about progress. Everyone has behaviors they'd like to change, but the path to improvement begins with compassion and curiosity. By examining the psychology behind these patterns, observing their triggers, and acknowledging their impact, we lay the groundwork for transformation.

Edison's early failures didn't define his legacy—they shaped it. By learning from his habits, he refined his approach to invention, eventually producing world-changing innovations. Similarly, your bad habits are not permanent obstacles; they are opportunities to grow. With self-awareness as your guide, you can uncover the hidden dynamics of your behaviors and take the first steps toward building a better, more intentional life.

The Art of Breaking Bad Habits – Strategies That Work

Breaking bad habits can feel like wrestling with an invisible force. These ingrained behaviors, often developed over years, seem to operate on autopilot, defying conscious effort to change. However, with the right strategies and a structured approach, even the most stubborn habits can be disrupted and replaced. The key lies in understanding the mechanics of change and employing proven methods to reshape your routines.

At the heart of breaking a bad habit is the principle of **substitution**. Habits don't simply vanish—they leave behind a void that needs to be filled. Substitution involves replacing an unwanted behavior with a more constructive one that serves the same purpose. For example, if someone habitually bites their nails when anxious, substituting the habit with a stress ball or a mindfulness exercise can satisfy the underlying need for relief without the negative consequences. This strategy is effective because it doesn't fight the habit loop directly; instead, it redirects it toward a healthier outcome.

The life of **Benjamin Franklin** offers a historical example of substitution in action. Known for his disciplined approach to self-improvement, Franklin identified his own vices and worked systematically to overcome them. One of his early challenges was a habit of argumentative behavior, which often alienated others. Recognizing this, Franklin substituted his confrontational tendencies with the habit of asking open-ended questions. This subtle yet profound shift allowed him to engage in productive dialogue, earning him a reputation as a wise and persuasive leader. Franklin's approach demonstrates how substitution can transform not only individual habits but also interpersonal relationships.

Another powerful method for breaking bad habits is **habit swapping**, a variation of substitution that leverages the existing structure of a habit loop. Instead of trying to eliminate a habit entirely, habit swapping modifies the routine while keeping the cue and reward intact. For example, if a person has the habit of eating junk food while watching TV, the cue (watching TV) and the reward (enjoyment) remain the same, but the routine can be swapped with a healthier alternative, such as snacking on fruits or drinking herbal tea. This method works because it aligns with the brain's natural preference for consistency, making the change feel less jarring.

The story of **Theodore Roosevelt** illustrates the power of habit swapping. As a young man, Roosevelt struggled with poor health and a sedentary lifestyle. Determined to improve, he swapped his inactive routines with vigorous physical activities like hiking, boxing, and horseback riding. Over time, these new habits not only transformed his health but also shaped his identity as a robust and adventurous leader. Roosevelt's example highlights how small, deliberate changes can cascade into significant personal growth.

While substitution and habit swapping are effective, they require a foundation of **self-awareness** and intentionality. One practical exercise for developing this foundation is the **habit disruption log**, where individuals track their habits for a week, noting the cues, routines, and rewards associated with each one. This practice brings unconscious behaviors into conscious awareness, providing the clarity needed to design meaningful interventions.

For example, someone who realizes they reach for their phone during moments of boredom might choose to disrupt this habit by substituting it with a quick walk or a few minutes of deep breathing. The act of logging creates a pause, breaking the automatic nature of the habit and opening the door for change.

Breaking bad habits also involves addressing the emotional and psychological barriers that sustain them. **Self-compassion** is a critical component of this process. All too often, people approach their bad habits with harsh self-criticism, which only reinforces feelings of failure and discouragement. A more effective approach is to view bad habits as learned behaviors rather than moral failings. This perspective fosters a growth mindset, encouraging experimentation and persistence rather than guilt or shame.

The life of **Mahatma Gandhi** provides a poignant example of self-compassion in the face of personal struggles. Despite his immense discipline and influence, Gandhi openly acknowledged his own shortcomings, including occasional lapses in temperance and patience. Rather than berating himself, he treated these moments as opportunities for reflection and growth. His ability to confront his imperfections with humility and resolve allowed him to model the principles of self-improvement for others.

Practical tools for self-compassion include journaling about setbacks, reframing negative thoughts, and seeking support from trusted friends or mentors. These practices create a safe space for change, reducing the emotional resistance that often accompanies efforts to break bad habits.

Finally, one of the most effective strategies for breaking bad habits is to focus on **environmental design**. Our surroundings play a powerful role in shaping our behaviors, often without our awareness. By modifying the environment to remove triggers for bad habits and introduce cues for positive ones, we can make change more effortless.

Consider the example of **James Clear**, author of **Atomic Habits**, who emphasizes the role of environment in habit formation. Clear recounts how he overcame a habit of unhealthy snacking by redesigning his kitchen—placing fruits and vegetables in visible locations while storing junk food out of sight. This simple change reduced the friction of choosing healthier options, making the new habit easier to adopt.

For readers, practical steps in environmental design might include rearranging the workspace to minimize distractions, creating designated areas for specific activities, or using reminders like sticky notes or phone alarms to reinforce desired behaviors. These small adjustments can have an outsized impact, transforming the environment from a source of temptation into a support system for growth.

Ultimately, the art of breaking bad habits lies in approaching the process with patience, creativity, and persistence. Substitution, habit swapping, self-awareness, self-compassion, and environmental design are not quick fixes—they are tools for sustainable transformation. By experimenting with these strategies and tailoring them to individual circumstances, it is possible to dismantle even the most entrenched habits and replace them with routines that align with our values and aspirations.

History reminds us that breaking bad habits is not just about eliminating the negative—it is about creating space for the positive. As Franklin, Roosevelt, and Gandhi demonstrate, the process of change is an opportunity to redefine ourselves, to rise above old patterns, and to build a life that reflects our highest potential. With determination and the right strategies, the habits that once held us back can become stepping stones toward a brighter future.

Building Better Habits – The Science of Positive Change

Building better habits is both an art and a science, requiring intention, persistence, and an understanding of the mechanisms that drive behavior. The journey begins with aligning habits to personal values and goals, ensuring they resonate with the life we aspire to create. This alignment not only provides motivation but also infuses the process with meaning, transforming routines into pathways for growth and self-discovery.

One powerful principle in habit formation is the idea that **small changes lead to significant transformations over time**. This is often referred to as the **compound effect**. Each small action, when repeated consistently, builds momentum, creating a ripple effect that amplifies results. For instance, committing to reading just ten pages a day may seem trivial, but over a year, it results in completing more than 3,500 pages—a feat that could include several life-changing books.

The story of **James Clear,** author of *Atomic Hab-*

its, provides a contemporary example of how small changes can yield substantial outcomes. Clear emphasizes starting with "atomic habits" — tiny, manageable actions that are easy to integrate into daily life. His approach stems from the understanding that habits are not just about what we do; they are about who we become. By consistently practicing small actions, we begin to see ourselves as the type of person who embodies those behaviors, reinforcing the habit at both a behavioral and identity level.

Visualization and affirmation are two additional tools that play a critical role in building better habits. Visualization involves imagining the desired outcome in vivid detail, creating a mental blueprint that guides action. This technique taps into the brain's capacity to simulate experiences, strengthening the neural pathways associated with the habit. For example, an aspiring runner might visualize themselves crossing the finish line of a marathon, feeling the exhilaration and pride of the accomplishment. This mental rehearsal makes the goal feel tangible and achievable, increasing motivation to take the necessary steps.

Affirmations, on the other hand, involve using positive self-statements to reinforce commitment and belief. These statements, such as "I am disciplined and capable of achieving my goals," help counteract self-doubt and negative thought patterns. By repeating affirmations regularly, individuals create a mental environment that supports their habits, fostering resilience and confidence.

History offers numerous examples of individuals who harnessed visualization and affirmation to achieve transformative change. Consider **Arnold Schwarzenegger**, who, long before becoming a world champion bodybuilder, visualized himself achieving that very title. He immersed himself in the identity of a champion, aligning his habits — daily training, disciplined nutrition, and relentless focus — with his vision. This alignment between visualization, affirmation, and action propelled him to success not only in bodybuilding but also in acting and politics.

For readers seeking to build better habits, the first step is to identify behaviors that align with their core values and aspirations. This process involves reflection and goal-setting, as well as asking critical questions:

- What kind of person do I want to become?

- What habits would support that identity?

- How can I break the goal into actionable, manageable steps?

These questions shift the focus from outcomes to identity, emphasizing the process of becoming rather than merely achieving.

One practical strategy for building habits is the **implementation intention** technique, which involves specifying when, where, and how a habit will occur. For example, instead of saying, "I will exercise more," an implementation intention might be, "I will go for a 30-minute walk at 7 a.m. every weekday." This level of specificity reduces ambiguity and creates a clear plan for action, making it easier to follow through.

Real-world examples highlight the power of this approach. **Barack Obama**, during his presidency, used structured routines to balance his demanding schedule. His habits, such as daily exercise and a consistent bedtime, were meticulously planned to support his physical health and mental clarity. These habits were not arbitrary — they were carefully chosen to align with his goal of leading with focus and resilience.

Another critical element of building better habits is creating a **reward system** that reinforces positive behavior. Rewards can be intrinsic, such as the satisfaction of completing a task, or extrinsic, such as a small treat or a celebratory ritual. The key is to associate the habit with a positive outcome, strengthening the brain's reward loop and increasing the likelihood of repetition.

Consider the example of **Serena Williams**, who attributes much of her success to her disciplined habits, including rigorous training, mental preparation, and strategic rest. For Williams, the intrinsic reward of mastering her craft and the extrinsic rewards of championships and accolades worked together to sustain her habits over decades. Her story underscores the importance of designing habits that are not only effective but also fulfilling.

In addition to rewards, accountability plays a

vital role in habit formation. Sharing goals with a trusted friend, mentor, or community creates a sense of responsibility and support. Whether it's a workout partner, a writing group, or an online forum, accountability strengthens commitment and provides encouragement during moments of doubt.

For modern readers, tools like habit-tracking apps, progress journals, or visual cues can serve as practical aids in building accountability. Tracking progress creates a sense of momentum, while visual cues—such as a calendar marked with daily successes—provide a tangible reminder of consistency.

Ultimately, building better habits is about designing systems that make success inevitable. It's not enough to rely on willpower or motivation, which are often fleeting. Instead, the focus should be on creating environments, routines, and mindsets that support the desired behavior effortlessly. Whether it's arranging the kitchen to prioritize healthy eating, setting up a distraction-free workspace, or using alarms to remind you of key habits, these systems simplify the process, reducing friction and increasing consistency.

The science of positive change teaches us that habits are not fixed—they are malleable, responsive to intention and effort. By aligning habits with our values, using tools like visualization and affirmation, and designing systems that support success, we can reshape our lives in meaningful ways. The journey may begin with small steps, but as these steps accumulate, they lead to profound transformation, creating a life that reflects the best version of ourselves.

Staying the Course – Tools for Long-Term Success

Building better habits is an essential step toward self-improvement, but the true challenge lies in maintaining those habits over the long term. Staying the course requires persistence, adaptability, and a system of strategies that make habits resilient to the ups and downs of life. By embracing tools for habit reinforcement and understanding the exponential benefits of consistency, we can turn fleeting changes into lifelong transformations.

One of the most effective tools for maintaining progress is **habit stacking**. This strategy involves linking a new habit to an existing one, creating a sequence that feels natural and automatic. For instance, someone aiming to develop a gratitude practice might add it to their morning coffee routine, taking a moment to reflect on three things they're thankful for while sipping their coffee. Habit stacking works because it leverages the stability of established routines, reducing the mental effort required to adopt new behaviors.

The concept of habit stacking can be traced to the rituals of historical figures like **Benjamin Franklin**, who famously maintained a daily schedule that integrated work, reflection, and self-improvement. Franklin's ability to stack habits—combining moments of quiet reflection with practical tasks—allowed him to maximize his time and sustain his commitments over decades. His method illustrates the importance of structuring habits in ways that feel seamless, ensuring their longevity.

Another critical tool for staying the course is **habit tracking**, a method of recording progress to create a sense of accountability and momentum. Tracking habits can be as simple as marking an "X" on a calendar each day the habit is completed or using a journal to document progress. The visual representation of consistency serves as both a motivator and a reminder, reinforcing the habit and making it harder to skip.

Habit tracking has been embraced by leaders and innovators throughout history. **Jerry Seinfeld**, the legendary comedian, used a habit-tracking method he called "Don't Break the Chain" to maintain his writing practice. Seinfeld would mark each day he wrote jokes on a calendar, creating a visible chain of success. His goal was simple: keep the chain unbroken. This technique highlights the psychological power of progress—each day of success strengthens the commitment to continue.

While tools like habit stacking and tracking are invaluable, maintaining habits over the long term also requires a mindset of **persistence and adaptability**. Life is unpredictable, and even the most well-intentioned routines can be disrupted by unexpected events. The key is to approach setbacks with resilience, viewing them not as failures but as opportunities to adjust and re-commit.

The story of **Helen Keller** exemplifies this principle. Keller, who overcame the challenges of being both blind and deaf, built habits of continuous learning and communication that transformed her life. Yet her journey was not without setbacks. Each new challenge required her to adapt her routines and find creative solutions. Keller's persistence in the face of adversity demonstrates that habits are not static—they are dynamic, evolving with our circumstances and needs.

To cultivate this mindset, it's helpful to set realistic expectations and embrace the idea of **progress over perfection**. Habits are not about flawless execution but about consistent effort. Missing a day or encountering a setback doesn't erase progress; it's simply a part of the process. The goal is to get back on track as quickly as possible, maintaining momentum over the long haul.

Another strategy for sustaining habits is to connect them to a larger purpose or vision. When habits are tied to meaningful goals, they gain a sense of significance that motivates continued effort. For example, a habit of daily exercise might be linked to the goal of maintaining health to spend more time with loved ones or pursue a passion. This connection transforms the habit from a mundane task into a vital part of a greater mission.

Mahatma Gandhi exemplified the power of purpose-driven habits. His daily routines, from spinning cotton to practicing meditation, were not merely personal disciplines—they were acts of resistance and expressions of his commitment to self-reliance and nonviolence. By tying his habits to his larger vision of social change, Gandhi sustained them even under the most challenging circumstances.

In addition to purpose, the role of **community and accountability** cannot be overstated. Habits thrive in supportive environments where others share or reinforce the commitment to change. Whether it's a running group, a book club, or an online community, being part of a network provides encouragement, feedback, and a sense of shared responsibility. These connections amplify motivation and create a buffer against setbacks.

Modern tools like habit-tracking apps and social accountability platforms make it easier than ever to build and maintain supportive communities. For instance, fitness apps that allow users to join challenges or share progress with friends create a sense of camaraderie and friendly competition, making habits more enjoyable and sustainable.

Finally, staying the course requires an understanding of the **exponential benefits of persistence**. Habits, much like investments, compound over time. The initial gains may seem small, but as consistency builds, the results become increasingly significant. This concept is vividly illustrated by the story of **Warren Buffett**, whose disciplined habits of saving, investing, and continuous learning led to unparalleled financial success. Buffett's life demonstrates that small, consistent actions, repeated over decades, create extraordinary outcomes.

For readers seeking to maintain their habits, it's helpful to visualize this compounding effect. Each small action—whether it's writing a single paragraph, practicing a skill for ten minutes, or preparing a healthy meal—contributes to a larger trajectory of growth and success. By focusing on the long-term impact rather than immediate results, it becomes easier to stay committed.

In conclusion, staying the course with habits is not about willpower alone—it's about creating systems and mindsets that support long-term success. Habit stacking, tracking, persistence, purpose, community, and an appreciation for exponential growth are the tools that transform fleeting efforts into enduring change. By embracing these strategies, we can ensure that the habits we build not only endure but also lead us toward the life we envision.

As Franklin, Keller, Gandhi, and Buffett remind us, habits are the scaffolding of achievement, the daily choices that shape our future. With patience, resilience, and the right tools, we can stay the course, transforming small actions into profound legacies.

CHAPTER 7: COLLECTIVE HABITS – THE POWER OF GROUP ROUTINES

Shared Habits in History – The Foundation of Synergy

Throughout history, collective habits have acted as the glue binding individuals into cohesive groups capable of extraordinary achievements. These shared routines not only foster unity and accountability but also amplify the strengths of individuals, enabling groups to achieve far more than the sum of their parts. From disciplined armies to groundbreaking artistic movements, the power of collective habits is evident in the lasting impact of these groups on the world.

One of the most striking examples of shared habits shaping a group's success is found in the **Roman legions**, the backbone of one of history's greatest empires. The discipline and effectiveness of these soldiers stemmed largely from their shared routines, meticulously drilled into them during training. Every soldier was expected to adhere to a rigorous schedule that included physical conditioning, weapon practice, and the construction of defensive fortifications. These habits, performed consistently and collectively, ensured that the legions functioned as a single, well-oiled machine.

The power of these shared habits extended beyond the battlefield. Roman soldiers participated in communal activities, such as shared meals and rituals, which strengthened their bonds and instilled a sense of purpose. This cohesion was essential for their success, especially in the high-stakes environment of military campaigns. The legions' routines not only kept them physically prepared but also created a culture of trust and reliability, where every soldier knew they could depend on their comrades to uphold the same standards.

The legacy of the Roman legions underscores an essential truth about collective habits: they create **synergy**. When individuals align their actions with those of the group, the resulting harmony generates an energy far greater than what any one person could achieve alone. This principle extends beyond military contexts, shaping artistic and scientific collaborations that have redefined human potential.

Consider the **Impressionist painters** of 19th-century France, a group that revolutionized the art world through their shared habits of experimentation and collaboration. Painters like Claude Monet, Edgar Degas, and Pierre-Auguste Renoir gathered regularly to critique each other's work, share techniques, and discuss emerging ideas. These gatherings were not casual encounters—they were rituals that reinforced their commitment to pushing the boundaries of traditional art.

The Impressionists' collective habits of working en plein air (painting outdoors), experimenting with light and color, and embracing spontaneity created a distinctive style that challenged the rigid conventions of the time. By holding one another accountable to their shared vision, they fostered an environment of mutual growth and innovation. Their habits became the foundation for a movement that continues to influence art to this day.

Similarly, the power of collective habits is evident in scientific communities, where shared routines enable breakthroughs that transform our understanding of the world. The **Manhattan Project**, which brought together some of the greatest minds of the 20th century to develop nuclear technology, relied heavily on shared habits of collaboration, rigorous experimentation, and disciplined problem-solving. Scientists like J. Robert Oppenheimer, Enrico Fermi, and Richard Feynman worked in highly structured environments where routines were designed to maximize efficiency and creativity. Despite the ethical debates surrounding the project, its success illustrates how collective habits can unite diverse talents to achieve unprecedented goals.

For modern readers, these historical examples offer valuable insights into the benefits of shared habits. First, collective routines create **accountability**, as each member of the group feels a responsibility to uphold their role. In the Roman legions, a single soldier failing to perform their duties could jeopardize the safety of the entire unit. This sense of shared accountability motivates individuals to maintain high standards, knowing their actions contribute to a larger purpose.

Second, shared habits foster **cohesion** by providing a common framework for interaction. Whether it's soldiers marching in unison, artists gathering for critique sessions, or scientists adhering to a rigorous schedule, these routines create a sense of unity that strengthens the group's resolve. In a world where distractions and individualism often pull people apart, collective habits offer a way to reconnect and align efforts toward a common goal.

The practical implications of these lessons are profound. For those seeking to create or join groups with shared habits, the key lies in establishing routines that are both meaningful and sustainable. This begins with a clear **shared purpose**, as seen in the Impressionists' vision of redefining art or the Roman legions' commitment to defending their empire. Purpose gives the habits context, making them more than mere routines—it transforms them into acts of alignment with a greater mission.

Another critical factor is **consistency**. Collective habits thrive on regularity, as this reinforces their importance and ensures their integration into the group's culture. Scheduling regular meetings, rituals, or activities creates a rhythm that becomes second nature, reducing resistance and increasing participation.

Finally, successful collective habits require

adaptability. The best routines are those that evolve with the needs of the group, accommodating new challenges and opportunities without losing sight of their core purpose. This flexibility was evident in the Impressionists' willingness to embrace new techniques and the Roman legions' ability to adapt their strategies to different terrains and enemies.

Shared habits are not just relics of history—they are tools we can use to build better communities, organizations, and movements today. Whether it's a family establishing a routine for quality time, a workplace creating rituals to foster collaboration, or a social movement aligning around shared actions, the principles of collective habits remain timeless.

In the end, the power of collective habits lies in their ability to transform individuals into a unified force, capable of achieving what would be impossible alone. By studying the examples of the Roman legions, the Impressionist painters, and other historical groups, we can draw inspiration for cultivating shared routines that bring out the best in ourselves and those around us. These habits remind us that, when we act together with purpose and discipline, we can create legacies that endure far beyond our time.

Team Productivity – Lessons from High-Performing Groups

In the realm of human achievement, the power of teamwork is undeniable. High-performing teams accomplish feats that seem almost miraculous, blending diverse talents into a seamless whole. Behind this magic lies a simple truth: productive teams thrive on shared habits. These routines form the backbone of trust, alignment, and momentum, enabling teams to overcome challenges and achieve extraordinary results.

Sports teams provide some of the most vivid examples of the power of collective habits. Consider the rituals and routines of **Olympic athletes**, who compete at the highest level of their sport. Beyond their individual training, Olympic teams often engage in shared practices designed to foster unity and synchronization. For example, relay teams not only perfect their individual sprints but also practice the handoff of the baton countless times. This seemingly small act—transferring the baton—requires precision, timing, and trust. Without a seamless handoff, even the fastest runners would fail. The collective habit of drilling this transition transforms the team into a cohesive unit, turning potential weak points into areas of strength.

The success of these teams is not just physical—it's psychological. Shared rituals, such as pre-game huddles or chants, create a sense of shared identity and purpose. These habits build trust, reminding every member that they are part of something larger than themselves. Trust, in turn, reduces friction and allows the team to focus on their shared goals. It is this alignment, born of shared routines, that turns a group of individuals into a synchronized force.

The corporate world offers similar lessons. Companies like **Pixar**, renowned for their creative output, attribute much of their success to team habits that foster collaboration and innovation. At Pixar, one of the most celebrated routines is the "Braintrust" meeting—a regular gathering where directors present their work in progress to a trusted group of peers. The purpose of these meetings is not to criticize but to offer candid, constructive feedback in an environment of mutual respect. This habit of open dialogue, practiced consistently across projects, ensures that every film benefits from the collective wisdom of the team.

The Braintrust exemplifies a core principle of productive teams: the importance of rituals that foster trust and alignment. By creating a safe space for honest communication, Pixar empowers its teams to take creative risks while staying grounded in shared goals. These meetings are more than a business practice—they are a habit that reinforces the company's culture of excellence and collaboration.

Another key lesson from high-performing teams is the role of **routine in managing energy and focus**. Teams that operate at peak performance understand the importance of balancing intense effort with periods of rest and reflection. Take the example of championship sports teams like the **Golden State Warriors**, who incorporate mindfulness and recovery routines into their training. Players engage in meditation, yoga, and other practices that help them stay mentally sharp and physically resilient. These habits not only enhance individual performance but also strengthen the team as a whole, ensuring that every member brings their best to the game.

For teams in any field, the challenge lies in designing habits that drive results while respecting the individuality of each member. A one-size-fits-all approach rarely works; instead, successful teams create routines that are flexible and adaptive. For example, a software development team might use daily stand-up meetings to align on priorities and address roadblocks. These short, focused check-ins become a shared habit that keeps the team on track without overwhelming their schedules.

To build effective team habits, it's essential to focus on three core elements: **clarity, consistency, and adaptability**.

- **Clarity** ensures that everyone understands the purpose and value of the habit. Without clarity, routines can feel arbitrary, leading to disengagement.

- **Consistency** establishes the habit as a non-negotiable part of the team's rhythm, reinforcing its importance.

- **Adaptability** allows the habit to evolve with the team's needs, ensuring it remains relevant and effective over time.

One strategy for fostering clarity and alignment is the use of **team charters**, which outline the group's shared goals, values, and expectations. These charters serve as a reference point, reminding members of their collective purpose and the habits that will help them achieve it. For example, a startup team might include habits like weekly brainstorming sessions or monthly check-ins on progress toward key metrics. By codifying these routines, the team creates a framework that supports both accountability and creativity.

Leadership plays a pivotal role in embedding team habits. Leaders who model the desired behaviors set the tone for the group, demonstrating the importance of consistency and commitment. This principle is evident in the leadership of figures like **John Wooden**, the legendary UCLA basketball coach. Wooden's teams were known not only for their championship titles but also for their disciplined habits, from meticulously organized practices to a focus on fundamentals like proper footwork. Wooden's leadership style emphasized the value of small, consistent actions, which became the foundation for his team's extraordinary success.

For modern readers, the lessons of high-performing teams offer practical guidance for improving group productivity. Whether you're leading a workplace team, a community organization, or a family, the principles remain the same: establish shared habits that align with your goals, foster trust through consistent rituals, and remain open to adaptation as circumstances evolve.

One actionable step is to start with a single team habit that addresses a specific need. For instance, if communication is a challenge, consider implementing a daily or weekly check-in meeting. If collaboration needs improvement, create a habit of shared brainstorming sessions or peer reviews. Over time, these habits will become ingrained, shaping the team's culture and enhancing its effectiveness.

Ultimately, the power of team productivity lies

in the synergy created by shared habits. As the examples of Olympic teams, Pixar, and other high-performing groups demonstrate, these routines are more than just practices—they are the building blocks of trust, alignment, and excellence. By cultivating habits that unite and empower, teams can achieve results that exceed their individual capabilities, leaving a legacy of collaboration and success.

Cultural Habits – Shaping Societies Through Routine

Cultural habits, the collective routines that define how societies function, hold immense power in shaping identity, fostering unity, and driving progress. From daily practices to deeply rooted traditions, these habits reflect the shared values of a community and influence how people interact with one another and the world. They are the invisible threads that weave individuals into a collective whole, enabling societies to flourish.

One striking example of cultural habits influencing a population is the **Japanese tea ceremony**, or *chanoyu*. This intricate ritual, steeped in Zen philosophy, represents much more than

the act of drinking tea—it is a cultural cornerstone emphasizing harmony, respect, purity,
and tranquility. Every element of the ceremony,
from the arrangement of the tea utensils to the
gestures of the host, is meticulously practiced,
reflecting the values of mindfulness and attention to detail. The repetition of this ritual reinforces these values, embedding them into the
fabric of Japanese society.

The tea ceremony also highlights how cultural
habits can create a sense of shared identity. By
participating in this ritual, individuals connect
not only with the present moment but also with
centuries of tradition, linking them to a collective heritage. This sense of continuity fosters
unity and pride, reminding participants of their
role in preserving and perpetuating their culture.

Another example of cultural habits shaping societies can be seen in the **monastic routines of
medieval Europe.** Monasteries were centers of
learning, agriculture, and spiritual practice, and
the daily habits of monks—prayer, study, and
labor—created a rhythm that influenced broader societal norms. These routines emphasized

discipline, devotion, and a balance between work and contemplation, values that resonated throughout medieval European culture. The habits of monastic communities not only sustained their members but also contributed to the preservation of knowledge and the spread of education during a time when much of the Western world faced instability.

Cultural habits also play a role in shaping how societies adapt to change. Consider the **Industrial Revolution**, a period that disrupted traditional routines and required the development of new habits to navigate an era of rapid innovation. The introduction of factory work, with its rigid schedules and repetitive tasks, fundamentally altered how people organized their days. While this shift brought challenges, it also introduced the concept of standardization, laying the groundwork for modern productivity. The shared routines of factory laborers, although demanding, created a sense of collective effort and progress, driving the growth of industries and economies.

However, the transformative power of cultural habits is not without its complexities. While they can foster unity and progress, these routines can also become obstacles to change if they are too rigidly held. Traditions that no longer serve the needs of a society may hinder innovation, creating tension between the desire for continuity and the necessity of adaptation.

One example of this tension is the **practice of foot binding in China**, a centuries-old tradition that symbolized beauty and social status but caused immense physical suffering. For generations, this cultural habit persisted despite its harmful effects, as it was deeply tied to identity and societal expectations. It was not until the late 19th and early 20th centuries, when reform movements challenged the practice, that foot binding began to decline. This shift highlights the difficulty of breaking entrenched cultural habits but also underscores the potential for progress when societies critically examine their traditions.

The interplay between cultural habits and identity can also be seen in how societies respond to external influences. The **Renaissance**, a period of cultural rebirth in Europe, was fueled by the exchange of ideas and practices between different regions and traditions. The adoption of new habits, such as the study of classical texts and the patronage of the arts, transformed European culture, leading to advancements in science, literature, and philosophy. This period illustrates how embracing change while preserving core values can lead to extraordinary achievements.

For modern readers, the lessons of cultural habits offer valuable insights into how routines shape collective identity and progress. One takeaway is the importance of **mindful preservation**—honoring traditions that reflect a society's core values while remaining open to evolution. Practices like the Japanese tea ceremony demonstrate how rituals can provide a sense of stability and meaning, even in the face of change.

At the same time, it is crucial to recognize when cultural habits need to be reevaluated. This requires a willingness to ask difficult questions:

- Does this habit align with our current values and needs?

- Are there alternative routines that could better

serve our goals?

- How can we honor the past while embracing
the future?

Breaking or changing cultural habits is rarely
easy, as these routines are often tied to deeply
held beliefs and identities. However, as history
shows, societies that navigate this process with
care and intention can achieve remarkable progress. Whether it's the abolition of harmful practices like foot binding or the adoption of new
technologies during the Industrial Revolution,
the ability to adapt cultural habits is a hallmark
of resilience and growth.

Leaders play a pivotal role in this process, serving as stewards of cultural habits and agents of
change. By modeling routines that align with
shared values, leaders can inspire communities
to embrace habits that foster unity and progress.
This is evident in figures like **Mahatma Gandhi**,
whose daily habits of simplicity and nonviolence embodied the principles of his movement.
Gandhi's ability to align his personal routines
with the broader goals of Indian independence
demonstrates the power of cultural habits to

inspire collective action.

Ultimately, cultural habits are not just routines—they are expressions of identity, values, and vision. They shape how societies function, how they adapt to change, and how they envision their future. By understanding the power of these habits, individuals and communities can harness their potential to create a more cohesive and purposeful world. Whether through preserving meaningful traditions or embracing new routines, the journey of cultural habits is one of continuous evolution, reflecting the ever-changing needs and aspirations of humanity.

Creating Group Momentum – Building Routines That Last

Building and sustaining group momentum through collective habits is both an art and a science. The success of any group effort—whether a team, community, or movement—depends on routines that align individual actions with a shared purpose. When group habits are intentional, consistent, and adaptive, they create a powerful engine for long-term progress. However, the journey to establish and maintain these

habits requires thoughtful strategies, strong
leadership, and a willingness to overcome resistance.

One of the most important steps in creating
group momentum is to establish **clear and actionable routines** that everyone can commit
to. Clarity is essential because ambiguity leads
to inconsistency, which undermines trust and
cohesion. For instance, during the **American
Civil Rights Movement**, leaders like Martin
Luther King Jr. emphasized the importance of
nonviolent resistance as a collective habit. By
clearly defining the principles and actions associated with this approach—such as peaceful
marches, sit-ins, and boycotts—they created a
framework that united participants and amplified the movement's impact.

Clarity alone, however, is not enough. To ensure that group habits are sustainable, they
must also be **achievable and scalable**. Starting
small is often the best approach. For example, a
workplace team aiming to improve collaboration might begin by instituting a simple daily
check-in meeting. This routine, while modest,
establishes a foundation of communication and

accountability. Over time, the group can build on this habit by adding more complex practices, such as project retrospectives or brainstorming sessions. The incremental nature of this process ensures that habits are not overwhelming, making them more likely to endure.

Another crucial factor in building group momentum is the role of **leadership in modeling habits**. Leaders set the tone for the group by demonstrating the behaviors they wish to see. This principle is evident in the practices of **Mahatma Gandhi**, who embodied the ideals of simplicity, discipline, and self-reliance that he encouraged in his followers. Gandhi's personal habits, such as spinning his own clothes and fasting, served as a powerful example, inspiring others to adopt similar routines in support of India's independence movement. When leaders align their actions with the group's goals, they create a sense of authenticity and trust that strengthens collective commitment.

Leadership also plays a key role in addressing and overcoming **resistance to change**. Groups often face inertia, as individuals may be hesitant to adopt new habits due to fear of failure, discomfort, or skepticism about the benefits. Effective leaders anticipate these challenges and address them with empathy and strategic interventions. For example, they might highlight small early wins to demonstrate the value of the new routine or create opportunities for group members to provide feedback and feel heard. By fostering a culture of collaboration and adaptability, leaders can ease the transition and maintain momentum.

In addition to leadership, **shared accountability** is a powerful driver of group habits. When individuals know their actions contribute to a larger effort, they are more likely to stay committed. This principle is illustrated by the routines of **open-source software communities**, where developers from around the world collaborate to create and maintain projects. These groups rely on habits like regular code reviews, documentation updates, and scheduled releases. The shared accountability inherent in these routines ensures that everyone contributes to the project's success while benefiting from the collective effort.

Creating group momentum also requires an

understanding of **how to align individual goals with group objectives**. When people see how their personal aspirations connect to the collective mission, they are more motivated to participate. For instance, a fitness class that emphasizes individual progress while fostering a sense of camaraderie creates an environment where participants feel both supported and challenged. This alignment can be reinforced through recognition and celebration of achievements, whether it's acknowledging a team's successful project completion or celebrating milestones in a community initiative.

Adaptability is another critical element of sustaining group habits. As circumstances change, routines must evolve to remain relevant and effective. The history of the **Apollo space program** offers a compelling example of this principle. NASA's teams faced countless challenges in their quest to land humans on the moon, from technical failures to shifting political priorities. Despite these obstacles, they maintained momentum by continuously refining their processes and adapting their routines to new realities. This ability to pivot without losing sight of the overarching goal ensured the program's ultimate success.

Finally, the longevity of group habits depends on cultivating a sense of **ownership and empowerment** among participants. When individuals feel that they have a stake in shaping the group's routines, they are more likely to stay engaged and invested. This can be achieved through practices like collaborative decision-making, where group members contribute ideas and have a voice in setting priorities. Empowerment fosters a sense of agency, turning group habits into shared commitments rather than imposed obligations.

For readers seeking to build and sustain group momentum, there are several actionable steps to consider:

- **Start with a clear and compelling purpose.** Define why the habit matters and how it aligns with the group's values and goals.

- **Make the first steps manageable.** Begin with simple, achievable routines that build confidence and establish a foundation.

- **Lead by example.** Demonstrate the desired habits consistently, setting the standard for the group.

- **Celebrate progress.** Acknowledge milestones and achievements to reinforce commitment and morale.

- **Be open to feedback.** Encourage group members to share their perspectives and suggestions, fostering a culture of continuous improvement.

By following these principles, groups can create habits that not only drive immediate results but also build the resilience and adaptability needed for long-term success.

In conclusion, the power of group routines lies in their ability to transform individual actions into collective progress. Whether it's a social movement, a high-performing team, or a community initiative, the momentum generated by shared habits can achieve remarkable outcomes. By combining clarity, consistency, leadership, and adaptability, we can create routines that unite, inspire, and sustain groups in their pursuit of meaningful goals. Through these habits,

the potential for growth and achievement becomes limitless, proving that together, we are
greater than the sum of our parts.

CHAPTER 8: HABITS FOR A LIFETIME – SUSTAINING GROWTH AND FULFILLMENT

The Habit Journey – Growth Beyond the Immediate

Habits are not static. They grow, evolve, and adapt over time, reflecting the changing circumstances and aspirations of the individual. While habits often begin as small, deliberate actions, they can mature into powerful forces that shape not just a person's daily life but also their legacy. This journey from intention to transformation reveals the profound connection between habits and purpose—a dynamic interplay that can sustain growth and fulfillment across a lifetime.

The philosopher **Confucius**, whose teachings have guided millions, exemplifies the enduring power of habits. Confucius believed that virtue and wisdom could be cultivated through consistent practice. His daily routines, which included reflection, study, and disciplined action, were not arbitrary; they were rooted in a deeper purpose: the betterment of himself and society. For Confucius, habits were not ends in themselves but pathways to living a life aligned with his values of integrity, respect, and harmony. Over decades, these routines became second nature, reinforcing his role as a teacher and moral guide.

His life reminds us that habits, when tied to a clear purpose, gain a resilience that carries them through the ebb and flow of life.

The evolution of habits often mirrors the stages of personal growth. In the beginning, a habit may feel like a struggle—a conscious effort to integrate a new behavior into an established rhythm. Over time, however, repetition turns that effort into ease. Consider the story of **Beethoven**, who maintained a lifelong habit of meticulous composition. Each morning, he would rise early and prepare coffee with exactly sixty coffee beans, a practice that reflected his precision and discipline. Then, he would settle into his work, immersing himself in the world of sound and structure. This habit, repeated daily, allowed Beethoven to channel his creativity and navigate the immense challenges of his life, including his struggle with hearing loss. His routines were not just tools for productivity; they were anchors that provided stability and focus amid adversity.

The idea that habits evolve over time is also evident in the lives of individuals who adapt their routines to new goals or phases of life. **Eleanor**

Roosevelt, one of the most influential figures of the 20th century, offers a striking example. Early in her life, she adopted the habit of journaling—a practice that helped her process her thoughts and emotions. As she grew into her role as a First Lady and humanitarian, this habit became a foundation for her public speaking and writing. Through reflection and adaptation, her journaling evolved from a personal exercise to a powerful tool for advocacy and connection, enabling her to share her voice and inspire change.

These stories reveal a fundamental truth about the habit journey: it is not linear. Life's complexities often require adjustments, pauses, or even reinvention. The habits that serve us at one stage of life may need to be reimagined to align with new priorities or challenges. This adaptability is not a sign of failure but a testament to the dynamic nature of habits. It reflects a deeper awareness of how our routines support our goals and values over time.

To nurture habits that endure, it is essential to anchor them in a sense of **purpose and identity**. Habits rooted in superficial motivations are more likely to fade when circumstances change or initial enthusiasm wanes. In contrast, habits that align with a person's core values and aspirations gain a sense of permanence. For example, a teacher who views their habit of daily lesson planning not just as a task but as a commitment to their students' success is more likely to sustain that routine over decades. This connection between habits and purpose transforms routine actions into meaningful rituals, infusing them with resilience and longevity.

As habits evolve, they often reveal patterns of interconnected growth. One habit can spark a cascade of positive changes, leading to new routines that complement and reinforce the original behavior. This phenomenon is evident in the life of **Mahatma Gandhi** whose practice of daily spinning was more than an act of self-sufficiency. It became a symbol of resistance, simplicity, and unity, inspiring others to adopt habits that aligned with the broader movement for Indian independence. Gandhi's spinning wheel reminds us that even the simplest habits can grow into powerful expressions of collective purpose.

For modern readers, the habit journey offers a roadmap for lifelong growth and fulfillment. It begins with small, deliberate actions, anchored in a clear sense of purpose. Over time, these habits evolve, adapting to new goals and challenges while maintaining their connection to the individual's core values. This evolution requires patience, reflection, and a willingness to adjust, but it also offers unparalleled rewards: a life shaped by intentionality and enriched by the steady pursuit of what truly matters.

One practical way to nurture the evolution of habits is through periodic **reflection and evaluation**. By taking time to assess the effectiveness of routines, individuals can identify what is working, what needs adjustment, and how their habits align with their current goals. Questions like "What purpose does this habit serve?" and "How has this habit supported my growth?" can illuminate the path forward, ensuring that routines remain relevant and meaningful.

The habit journey is not about perfection; it is about progress. It is a lifelong process of learning, adapting, and striving toward a life of purpose and fulfillment. As the stories of Confucius,

Beethoven, and Eleanor Roosevelt show, habits are more than mere routines—they are expressions of identity, reflections of values, and catalysts for transformation. By embracing the dynamic nature of habits, we can unlock their full potential, creating a life that evolves and grows in harmony with our deepest aspirations.

The Role of Reflection – Learning and Adjusting Along the Way

Habits are not static, nor should they be. While consistency is a hallmark of effective routines, it is through periodic reflection that habits are refined and aligned with evolving goals and circumstances. This practice of looking inward, evaluating progress, and making thoughtful adjustments is the cornerstone of sustained growth and fulfillment. Reflection transforms habits from rote actions into meaningful rituals, ensuring they continue to serve the individual's higher purpose over time.

The importance of reflection is evident in the writings of **Benjamin Franklin**, who developed one of history's most methodical approaches to self-improvement. Franklin famously maintained a daily journal in which he assessed his progress on thirteen virtues he sought to embody, such as humility, temperance, and industry. Each evening, he reflected on the day's events, noting where he had succeeded and where he had faltered. This process of self-assessment allowed Franklin to refine his habits continually, ensuring they aligned with his personal values and aspirations. His journal was not just a record of his life—it was a tool for growth, a mirror that revealed both his achievements and opportunities for improvement.

Reflection also plays a vital role in identifying the subtle shifts that can make a habit more sustainable or impactful. Consider the story of **Maya Angelou**, the celebrated poet and author, who maintained a habit of writing every morning in a rented hotel room. Over time, Angelou realized that her creative process benefited from small adjustments—like choosing a room with a simple, uncluttered environment or setting specific time limits for her writing sessions. These refinements, discovered through reflection, enhanced her productivity and helped her craft works that continue to inspire generations.

In the modern context, tools like **journaling** and **self-assessments** offer practical ways to engage in reflective practice. Journaling, as Franklin and Angelou demonstrated, provides a structured way to record experiences, track progress, and identify patterns. For those new to the practice, a simple prompt such as "What habit served me well today, and why?" can spark meaningful insights. Over time, this habit of journaling becomes a space for celebrating wins, acknowledging challenges, and envisioning the next steps.

Self-assessments, on the other hand, offer a more systematic approach to reflection. By periodically asking questions like "What habits are supporting my current goals?" and "What adjustments could improve my routines?" individuals can take a bird's-eye view of their progress. These assessments are particularly useful during transitions—whether it's starting a new job, moving to a new city, or entering a different phase of life. By pausing to reflect, individuals ensure their habits remain relevant and effective in changing circumstances.

The process of reflection is not only about looking back but also about looking forward. It invites a mindset of **continuous improvement**, where small adjustments build momentum over time. For example, a runner aiming to build endurance might start with a daily habit of jogging a mile. Through reflection, they may discover that adding a warm-up routine reduces fatigue or that running with a friend increases their motivation. These small tweaks, while seemingly minor, compound into significant progress, reinforcing the habit's long-term sustainability.

The role of reflection extends beyond the individual to encompass teams, organizations, and even entire societies. **The Apollo space program** offers a powerful example of reflection driving collective progress. After the tragedy of Apollo 1, where a cabin fire claimed the lives of three astronauts, NASA undertook an exhaustive review of its practices and procedures. This reflective process led to critical changes in safety protocols, engineering designs, and team communication. These adjustments not only salvaged the program but also laid the foundation for one of humanity's greatest achievements: landing on the moon. The Apollo program demonstrates how reflection, even in the face of setbacks, can transform failure into opportunity and pave the way for extraordinary success.

Reflection also cultivates **self-awareness**, a crucial ingredient for meaningful habit formation. Without awareness, it is easy to fall into patterns of behavior that may feel comfortable but ultimately fail to serve one's goals. By taking time to reflect, individuals can identify habits that no longer align with their values or aspirations, creating space for new, more purposeful routines. This process requires honesty and humility—a willingness to acknowledge what isn't working and the courage to make changes.

One practical example of this is the concept of **habit stacking**, popularized by behavioral experts. Reflection allows individuals to identify existing routines and consider how new habits might seamlessly integrate into their lives. For instance, someone who already enjoys a morning cup of coffee might add a habit of gratitude journaling during that time. This approach not only builds on existing momentum but also ensures that new habits align with the rhythms of daily life.

For readers seeking to incorporate reflection into their habit journey, the following practices can serve as starting points:

- **Schedule regular check-ins.** Set aside time weekly or monthly to review your habits, noting what's working and what could be improved.

- **Ask meaningful questions.** Focus on prompts that encourage self-awareness, such as "How does this habit support my values?" or "What small change could make this habit more effective?"

- **Celebrate progress.** Reflection is not just about identifying areas for improvement—it's also about acknowledging successes and reinforcing positive behaviors.

Ultimately, the role of reflection is not to impose perfection but to foster intentionality. It transforms habits from static routines into dynamic practices, allowing them to grow and evolve alongside the individual. Whether through journaling, self-assessments, or moments of quiet introspection, reflection ensures that habits remain aligned with purpose, adaptable to change, and capable of driving sustained growth.

In conclusion, reflection is the compass that guides the habit journey, offering direction and clarity in an ever-changing landscape. By learning and adjusting along the way, individuals can ensure their routines remain not just effective but also meaningful. As Franklin, Angelou, and the countless others who have embraced reflection show us, this practice is not merely an exercise in self-awareness—it is a pathway to lifelong growth and fulfillment.

Celebrating Progress – Acknowledging Wins Big and Small

Habits thrive on momentum, and few things build momentum as effectively as celebration. Recognizing achievements, no matter how small, serves as a powerful reinforcement for behavior, linking effort with positive emotions and encouraging continued progress. Celebration transforms routine milestones into meaningful moments, embedding motivation and gratitude into the habit journey. It is not just a reward—it is an essential part of sustaining growth and fulfillment.

The psychological benefits of celebrating progress are well-documented. Research shows that acknowledging achievements releases **dopamine**, a neurotransmitter associated with pleasure and motivation. This chemical response reinforces the neural pathways linked to the habit, making it more likely to be repeated. For example, consider the impact of acknowledging the completion of a daily workout. A simple moment of reflection, such as saying, "I'm proud of myself for showing up today," strengthens the habit by associating it with feelings of accomplishment and self-worth.

Celebration also fosters a sense of momentum. **Sir Edmund Hillary**, one of the first climbers to summit Mount Everest, understood the importance of recognizing progress during his monumental journey. Each milestone—reaching a base camp, navigating a difficult passage—was celebrated with his team, not only as a sign of achievement but also as a way to refocus and recharge for the challenges ahead. These moments of gratitude and recognition provided the psychological fuel needed to keep going, even when the ultimate goal seemed distant.

For individuals and teams alike, the act of celebrating milestones cultivates a culture of positivity and resilience. **The Apollo 11 mission** offers a compelling example. The NASA teams behind the historic moon landing celebrated each successful test and launch as a collective victory, creating a sense of shared purpose and camaraderie. These celebrations, often modest in nature, helped sustain morale during the grueling and uncertain journey to achieving one of humanity's greatest accomplishments. By acknowledging both big wins and small steps forward, the team maintained the momentum needed to reach their ultimate goal.

Gratitude plays a key role in effective celebration. When we pause to appreciate our progress, we shift our focus from what remains undone to what has already been achieved. This mindset cultivates a sense of abundance and satisfaction, counteracting the tendency to downplay accomplishments in favor of future ambitions. **Maya Angelou**, known for her habit of writing every day, often emphasized the importance of celebrating the act of creation itself, regardless of the outcome. For Angelou, gratitude for the process was as vital as recognition of the result, reinforcing her lifelong commitment to her craft.

Incorporating celebration into a habit routine can take many forms, from small, personal gestures to more elaborate expressions of recognition. For individuals, a simple act such as pausing to reflect on progress at the end of the day or sharing a milestone with a friend can create a sense of accomplishment. Teams can benefit from rituals like ringing a bell to mark a sale, hosting a weekly meeting to share wins, or organizing a group outing to celebrate collective success.

One effective method for sustaining habits through celebration is to tie rewards to specific milestones. For example, an individual who has maintained a habit of reading 20 pages daily might reward themselves with a new book after finishing three. A team working on a long-term project might celebrate the completion of each phase with a small party or recognition ceremony. These celebrations not only mark progress but also provide a tangible reminder of the value of consistent effort.

It is also important to celebrate progress in a way that aligns with the values and goals underlying the habit. For instance, someone cultivating a habit of healthy eating might celebrate a milestone by preparing a special nutritious meal rather than indulging in a behavior that contradicts their goals. This alignment reinforces the habit's purpose and keeps the celebration meaningful and supportive of long-term growth.

Reflection enhances the power of celebration, transforming it from a fleeting moment of joy into a meaningful ritual. Taking time to consider what made the milestone possible, who contributed to the success, and how the experience aligns with one's broader aspirations adds depth to the celebration. This reflective practice also provides insights for sustaining momentum and identifying opportunities for further improvement.

For those seeking to embrace celebration as a habit, it is worth noting that perfection is not a prerequisite for progress. Even partial success or incremental improvement deserves acknowledgment. This perspective shifts the focus from achieving an ideal outcome to valuing the effort and persistence behind every step forward. Such an approach encourages resilience, fostering a mindset that views setbacks not as failures but as opportunities for learning and growth.

Ultimately, celebrating progress is about more than just marking time—it is about creating a narrative of success, gratitude, and purpose. It transforms the habit journey from a series of isolated actions into a cohesive story of growth and achievement. By recognizing wins big and small, we build a foundation of positivity and motivation that sustains us through challenges and propels us toward fulfillment.

In conclusion, the practice of celebrating progress enriches the habit journey, providing motivation, gratitude, and perspective. Whether through small personal rituals or collective acts of recognition, celebration infuses habits with meaning and joy, ensuring they remain a source of inspiration and growth. As we celebrate our milestones, we not only honor our achievements but also reaffirm our commitment to the habits that shape our lives and the purpose they serve.

Legacy Through Habits – Inspiring the Next Generation

Habits are not confined to the individual—they echo far beyond, shaping the lives of others and leaving a legacy that endures. Every action, repeated consistently, creates ripples that influence those around us. Whether it's within a family, a community, or even across generations, habits possess the power to inspire, teach, and guide the future.

Consider the example of **Mahatma Gandhi**, whose habit of daily reflection and nonviolent resistance left an indelible mark on history. Gandhi's steadfast commitment to his principles was not just a personal practice—it became a model for millions striving for justice. His routines of simplicity, meditation, and public fasting were rooted in a profound belief in nonviolence, and these habits transcended his lifetime, inspiring movements for civil rights and freedom across the globe. The impact of Gandhi's habits reminds us that the routines we cultivate today can serve as a foundation for transformation long after we are gone.

Historical figures often leave behind enduring habits that influence generations. **Benjamin Franklin**, for example, developed a daily schedule that emphasized industry, order, and self-improvement. His habit of planning each day with precision, balanced by moments for reflection and learning, inspired not only his contemporaries but also countless individuals seeking guidance on productivity and purpose. Franklin's legacy lives on in the principles he documented, which continue to resonate in modern frameworks for personal and professional success.

The ripple effects of habits are perhaps most evident in the realm of mentorship and leadership. **Eleanor Roosevelt**, one of the most influential figures of the 20th century, exemplified the power of leading by example. Her habit of daily letter-writing not only kept her connected to the world but also created a vast archive of wisdom and encouragement. Roosevelt's consistent acts of outreach and reflection nurtured relationships and inspired action, influencing leaders who followed in her footsteps. Her habits underscored the importance of consistency and empathy in leaving a meaningful legacy.

At the heart of this legacy-building lies the concept of **modeling behavior**. The habits we practice visibly and consistently send a powerful message to those around us. Whether it's a parent showing their child the value of perseverance, a teacher demonstrating the importance of curiosity, or a leader embodying integrity, the routines we uphold become lessons for others. These habits create a framework for others to emulate, fostering values and practices that transcend the individual.

For readers seeking to cultivate habits with a lasting impact, it is essential to consider alignment with long-term values and goals. Habits that resonate with purpose are more likely to inspire and endure. Reflecting on questions such as "What values do I want to embody for others?" and "How can my habits support those values?" can help identify routines with the potential to create meaningful change.

The importance of habit legacy extends beyond individuals to families, organizations, and even entire societies. Cultural traditions, for instance, are often rooted in collective habits that have been passed down through generations. The **Japanese tea ceremony**, with its emphasis on mindfulness, respect, and simplicity, illustrates how shared routines can preserve cultural identity while fostering connection and reflection. These rituals, practiced over centuries, continue to offer guidance and inspiration in a rapidly changing world.

At an organizational level, the habits instilled by founders or leaders often define the ethos of their enterprises. **Howard Schultz**, the visionary behind Starbucks, emphasized the habit of creating a welcoming environment, both for customers and employees. This practice of fostering a "third place" between home and work became a cornerstone of the company's culture, influencing not just its success but also its impact on the broader business world. Schultz's legacy demonstrates how intentional habits can shape not only immediate outcomes but also enduring values.

Building a habit legacy also involves recognizing and celebrating the contributions of others. By acknowledging the habits and practices that inspire us, we create a sense of continuity and gratitude. For example, reflecting on the guidance of a mentor or the traditions of a family can deepen our understanding of how habits connect us across time and space. This recognition reinforces the idea that we are both recipients and creators of legacy, part of a larger tapestry of influence and growth.

For those inspired to leave a legacy through habits, consider the following steps:

1. **Identify core values.** Reflect on what matters most and how habits can align with those values.

2. **Model consistency.** Lead by example, demonstrating the power of routines to those around you.

3. **Share your journey.** Document your habits and insights, whether through writing, conversation, or mentorship.

4. **Encourage others.** Support those seeking to develop their own habits, creating a culture of growth and mutual inspiration.

The act of thinking about legacy invites a broader perspective on habits, shifting the focus from immediate benefits to long-term impact. It challenges us to consider how our daily actions contribute to the larger story of our lives and the lives we touch. Whether through small, quiet routines or bold, transformative practices, the habits we cultivate carry the potential to inspire and uplift others.

In conclusion, habits are not merely tools for personal growth—they are bridges to the future. By cultivating routines that align with our values and sharing them with others, we create a legacy of inspiration and purpose. As Gandhi, Franklin, Roosevelt, and countless others have shown, the habits we uphold today can shape the world of tomorrow, leaving behind a testament to resilience, wisdom, and humanity.

CONCLUSION: THE ENDURING POWER OF HABITS

Throughout the course of this book, we have explored the profound ways in which habits shape our lives, define our legacies, and propel us toward growth and fulfillment. From the smallest daily routines to the most ambitious undertakings, habits are the invisible threads that weave together the tapestry of our existence. They reflect who we are, influence who we become, and hold the potential to transform our future.

But beyond their capacity to create structure and efficiency, habits are deeply personal and infinitely adaptable. They are tools of empowerment, offering us a pathway to take control of our lives in an unpredictable world. As we conclude this journey, let us reflect on the themes and lessons that have guided our exploration of habits and their immense potential.

The Foundational Role of Habits

At the heart of every meaningful endeavor lies a set of foundational habits—those small, consistent actions that serve as the building blocks of success. As we discussed in the early chapters, habits are more than mere routines; they are the embodiment of our values and aspirations. By choosing habits that align with our goals and virtues, we lay a solid foundation for resilience and growth.

Consider the wisdom of the great minds we have examined: Aristotle's belief that excellence is not an act but a habit, Gandhi's steadfast commitment to nonviolence, and Franklin's meticulous approach to self-improvement. Their habits were not arbitrary but intentional, reflecting their deepest convictions and enabling them to navigate challenges with purpose.

The Science of Transformation

Understanding the science behind habits has been a crucial step in our journey. The habit loop—comprising the cue, routine, and reward—reminds us that habits are not fixed but malleable. With self-awareness and intentionality, we can rewire our brains to break unproductive patterns and replace them with constructive ones.

This transformation is not instantaneous but incremental. The compound effect teaches us that small changes, consistently applied, yield significant results over time. Whether it's cultivating a morning routine that sets the tone for the day or building resilience through keystone habits, the science affirms what experience often teaches: progress is a marathon, not a sprint.

Habits in Context

Habits do not exist in isolation; they are influenced by and, in turn, influence the people and environments around us. We saw this dynamic at play in collective habits—the shared routines that build trust, cohesion, and momentum within teams, families, and societies. From the discipline of the Roman legions to the synergy of high-performing creative groups, collective habits demonstrate the extraordinary power of alignment and collaboration.

Similarly, cultural habits reveal how shared

practices can preserve identity, foster connection, and inspire progress. The Japanese tea ceremony, for example, embodies mindfulness, respect, and harmony—values that transcend the individual and resonate across generations.

Resilience Through Change

Perhaps one of the most poignant lessons in this journey is the role of habits in navigating adversity. Life is inherently unpredictable, and challenges are inevitable. Yet, as figures like Nelson Mandela and Helen Keller have shown, habits can anchor us during turbulent times, providing stability and strength when everything else feels uncertain.

Building resilient habits is about more than perseverance; it is about adaptability. The ability to reassess, refine, and recommit to our routines ensures that they remain relevant and supportive, even as circumstances evolve. In this way, habits become not just tools for survival but catalysts for growth and reinvention.

The Habit Journey

As we move forward, it is essential to view habits not as static or rigid but as a journey of continuous learning and adjustment. Habits evolve alongside us, reflecting our changing priorities and aspirations. Periodic reflection allows us to evaluate their effectiveness, celebrate progress, and make necessary adjustments.

The act of celebration, often overlooked, is integral to sustaining motivation and joy. Recognizing milestones—big or small—reinforces our commitment and reminds us of the value of our efforts. It also deepens our sense of gratitude, both for the journey itself and for the people who support and inspire us along the way.

Leaving a Legacy

Finally, let us not forget the far-reaching impact of habits. The routines we cultivate today have the power to shape not only our own lives but also the lives of those around us. They create ripples that extend beyond our immediate circle, influencing future generations and contributing to the collective good.

Whether through mentorship, leadership, or

simply leading by example, we all have the capacity to leave a legacy of inspiration and purpose. As we reflect on the enduring habits of figures like Eleanor Roosevelt and Mahatma Gandhi, we are reminded that every action we take, no matter how small, holds the potential to create positive change.

Your Next Steps

As you close this book, take a moment to reflect on the habits that have brought you to this point. Which routines have served you well, and which could benefit from refinement or replacement? Consider the values and goals that matter most to you, and let them guide the habits you choose to cultivate moving forward.

Remember that every journey begins with a single step. You do not need to overhaul your life overnight; rather, focus on small, meaningful actions that align with your purpose. Trust in the process, and have faith in the power of consistency to bring about transformation.

A Final Thought

In the end, habits are not just about productivity or achievement—they are about living a life of intention, growth, and fulfillment. They are the bridges between who we are and who we aspire to be, offering us the opportunity to create a life of purpose and meaning.

As you embark on the next chapter of your journey, carry with you the lessons and insights from this exploration. Let them inspire you to approach each day with curiosity, commitment, and compassion—for yourself and for others. In the words of Confucius, "The journey of a thousand miles begins with a single step." Let that step be the beginning of a lifetime of intentional, transformative habits.

May your journey be one of discovery, growth, and profound fulfillment. The power to shape your life—and the world around you—lies within your habits. Go forth and make them count.

ACKNOWLEDGEMENT

This book would not have been possible without the guidance, inspiration, and support of many remarkable individuals.

To the countless thinkers, philosophers, and leaders whose wisdom has been a beacon throughout history, thank you for showing us the transformative power of habits. Your lives and lessons are the foundation of this work.

To my family, friends, and mentors, your encouragement has been the cornerstone of my journey. Thank you for your unwavering belief in my vision and for reminding me of the importance of perseverance and purpose.

To my readers, your curiosity and drive for

growth inspire me every day. This book is as much yours as it is mine, and I am deeply honored to be part of your journey toward lasting transformation.

Finally, a heartfelt thanks to the unseen forces of resilience, collaboration, and curiosity that have shaped this project and continue to shape our world.

May this book serve as a reflection of my gratitude and a source of inspiration for all who read it. Thank you.

ABOUT THE AUTHOR

Felix Grayson's journey into timeless wisdom began in childhood, captivated by the stories of philosophers, leaders, and visionaries who shaped the way we think and live. Growing up in a home filled with books, he spent countless hours exploring ideas that asked life's biggest questions—a curiosity that would later define his work.

After facing his own modern challenges—balancing ambition, uncertainty, and the search for meaning—Felix discovered that the wisdom of the past offers profound guidance for the present. This realization became the foundation for the *Stoned Philosopher* series: a collection dedicated to translating ancient insights into practical lessons for today's world.

Felix's writing is more than reflection—it's an invitation to dialogue with history's greatest minds. Through each book, he helps readers find clarity, resilience, and purpose in their own lives—one timeless idea at a time.

When not writing, Felix enjoys quiet contemplation, deep conversation, and exploring the endless pursuit of wisdom in everyday moments.